HITLER AND
NAZI GERMANY

QUESTIONS AND ANALYSIS IN HISTORY

Edited by Stephen J. Lee and Sean Lang

Other titles in this series:

Imperial Germany, 1871–1918
Stephen J. Lee

The Weimar Republic
Stephen J. Lee

The French Revolution
Jocelyn Hunt

Parliamentary Reform, 1785–1928
Sean Lang

The Spanish Civil War
Andrew Forrest

HITLER AND NAZI GERMANY

STEPHEN J. LEE

London and New York

First published 1998
by Routledge
11 New Fetter Lane, London EC4P 4EE

Simultaneously published in the USA and Canada
by Routledge
29 West 35th Street, New York, NY 10001

Reprinted 2000, 2001

Routledge is an imprint of the Taylor & Francis Group

Typeset in Grotesque and Perpetua by
Keystroke, Jacardanda Lodge, Wolverhampton
Printed and bound in Great Britain by
Clays Ltd, St Ives plc

British Library Cataloguing in Publication Data
A catalogue record for this book is available from the British Library

Library of Congress Cataloguing in Publication Data
has been applied for

ISBN 0–415–17988–2

CONTENTS

CONTENTS

SERIES PREFACE

Most history textooks now aim to provide the student with interpretation, and many also cover the historiography of a topic. Some include a selection of sources.

So far, however, there have been few attempts to combine *all* the skills needed by the history student. Interpretation is usually found within an overall narrative framework and it is often difficult to separate out the two for essay purposes. Where sources are included, there is rarely much guidance as to how to answer the questions on them.

The Questions and Analysis series is therefore based on the belief that another approach should be added to those which already exist. It has two main aims.

The first is to separate narrative from interpretation so that the latter is no longer diluted by the former. Most chapters start with a background narrative section containing essential information. This material is then used in a section focusing on analysis through a specific question. The main purpose of this is to help to tighten up essay technique.

The second aim is to provide a comprehensive range of sources for each of the issues covered. The questions are of the type which appear on examination papers, and some have worked answers to demonstrate the techniques required.

The chapters may be approached in different ways. The background narratives can be read first to provide an overall perspective, followed by the analyses and then the sources. The alternative method is to work through all the components of each chapter before going on to the next.

ACKNOWLEDGEMENTS

Author and publisher are grateful to the following for permission to reproduce copyright material:

V.R. Berghahn, *Modern Germany: Society, Economy and Politics in the Twentieth Century* (Cambridge University Press, first published 1982, edition used, 1995); J. Dulffer, *Nazi Germany 1933–1945: Faith and Annihilation* (trans. London 1966, Arnold); C. Fischer, *The Rise of the Nazis* (Manchester University Press); K. Hildebrand, *The Third Reich* (George Allen & Unwin); M. Housden, *Resistance and Conformity in the Third Reich* (London, Routledge 1997); Thomas Jones, *Lloyd George* (Cambridge, Mass., 1951); J. Laver, *Nazi Germany 1933–1945* (London, Hodder & Stoughton 1991); Louis P. Lochner (ed.) *The Goebbels Diaries 1942–3* (Washington, DC 1948); J. Noakes and G. Pridham eds: *Nazism 1919–1945* (University of Exeter Press 1983–8); D. Orlow, *The History of the Nazi Party*, vol. 2 (Newton Abbot, David and Charles, 1971); D.J.K. Peukert, *Inside Nazi Germany* (Penguin, 1982); J. Remak, *The Nazi Years* (Prentice-Hall, Englewood Cliffs, NJ 1969); L.L. Snyder, *The Weimar Republic* (Anvil Books, Princeton, NJ 1966); Otto Strasser: *Hitler and I* (London 1938, 1940).

While author and publisher have made every effort to contact copyright holders of material used in this volume, they would be grateful to hear from any they were unable to trace.

GLOSSARY

Anschluss: a term used to denote the union between Germany and Austria. Although specifically forbidden by the Treaty of Versailles (1919), this was carried out by Hitler in 1938.

BDM: *Bund Deutscher Mädel.* The League of German Maidens was that part of the Hitler Youth organisation catering for girls between the ages of fourteen and eighteen.

DAF: *Deutsche Arbeitsfront* or German Labour Front.

DDP: *Deutsche Demokratische Partei.* The Democratic Party was the left wing part of the liberal movement (*see also* DVP) which was a member of the original coalition from 1919 and a consistent supporter of the Weimar Republic. It weakened rapidly after 1930 and was banned in June 1933.

DJ: *Deutsches Jungvolk.* The German Young People were that part of the Hitler Youth movement catering for boys between ten and fourteen.

DNB: the German News Agency was one of the sub-chambers within the Ministry of People's Enlightenment and Propaganda.

DNVP: *Deutsche-Nationale Volkspartei.* The National Party was on the conservative right of the political spectrum. It was largely antagonistic to the Weimar Republic and favoured a more authoritarian regime. It collaborated closely with Hitler after 1929 but dissolved itself in 1933.

DVP: *Deutsche Volkspartei.* The People's Party was the more right wing of the two liberal parties. Its heyday was under the leadership of Stresemann. It declined rapidly after his death in 1929 and was ended in June 1933.

Einsatzgruppen: special task forces within the SS, largely responsible for the shooting of civilians in territories occupied by Germany.

Gau: a regional division of the NSDAP.

Gauleiter: leader of the Gau, responsible to Hitler.

Gestapo: *Geheime Stattspolizei* or Secret State Police. It was set up by Goering in Prussia in 1933 and was later drawn into the SS.

HJ: *Hitler Jugend.* The term 'Hitler Youth' has two meanings. It was used to denote the whole youth movement, but was also a specific part of that movement, intended for boys between fourteen and eighteen.

JM: *Jungmädelbund* the Young Maidens were that part of the Hitler Youth which catered for girls to the age of fourteen.

KdF: *Kraft durch Freude*, or Strength through Joy. This was a sub-division of the DAF, responsible for the use of leisure.

KPD: *Kommunistische Partei Deutschlands.* The Communist Party was formed by the merger of two splinter groups which broke away from the SPD as a result of conflicting views over the First World War. One was the Spartacus League and the other the Independent Socialists (USPD).

Land (plural *Länder*): a state or province within the German Reich.

Landtag: a parliament within a *Land*.

Lebensraum: the term 'living space' meant the acquisition of land and colonies for German settlement, largely in eastern Europe.

Mittlestand: lower middle class.

NSDAP: *Nationalsozialistische Partei Deutschlands.* The National Socialist German Workers' Party (usually abbreviated to Nazi) was the renamed version of the original DAP, set up in 1918.

NSLB: *Nationalsozialostische Lehrerbund*, or Nazi Teachers' League.

Panzer: heavy armoured division within the German army.

RAD: *Reichsarbeitsdienst*, or Reich Labour Service.

Reich: Empire. The First Reich was the Holy Roman Empire, ended in 1806; the Second Reich was ruled by the Kaisers between 1871 and 1918. The Third Reich was Nazi Germany (1933–45).

Reichsführer SS: the overall commander of the SS, a position occupied by Himmler.

Reichsrat: the second chamber of the German parliament, consisting of representatives appointed by the *Land* governments.

Reichstag: the main chamber of the German parliament, consisting of representatives elected by the people.

SA: *Sturmabteilung*, or stormtroopers, founded in 1921 and purged in the Night of the Long Knives (1934).

SD: *Sicherheitsdienst*, or security service within the SS – responsible largely for the collection of intelligence.

SDA: *Schönheit der Arbeit*, or Beauty of Labour, one of the sub-divisions of the DAF, responsible for working conditions and regulations.

SPD: *Sozialdemokratische Partei Deutschlands*, or Social Democratic Party. This was one of the two parties which survived from the Second Reich, although without its radical left wing, which formed the KPD instead. An important part of several of the coalition governments during the Weimar Republic, the SPD was eventually banned in July 1933.

SOPADE: The Social Democratic Party in exile was a movement to oppose the Nazi regime from abroad.

SS: *Schutzstaffeln*, or security squads. Formed in 1925 as an elite within the SA, it expanded rapidly under Himmler's leadership from 1929. As a result of the Night of the Long Knives (1934) it developed control over the whole police and security system, including the Gestapo.

Völkisch: literally 'concerning the people', but applied in a nationalist and racist sense.

Volksgemeinschaft: 'national community' which, in the Nazi sense, transcended class barriers, being based instead on racial identity.

Waffen SS: the military units of the SS, which served in the Wehrmacht.

Wehrmacht: the reorganised German army, which replaced the earlier *Reichswehr*.

Zentrum (Z): The Centre Party represented religious interests in the Weimar Republic – mainly, although not exclusively, Catholic. It was banned in June 1933.

1

THE RISE OF NAZISM

BACKGROUND NARRATIVE

The Nazi movement originated in Munich as the German Workers' Party (DAP), one of a number of *völkisch*, or radical fringe, groups established immediately after the end of the First World War. Hitler, previously an impoverished Austrian artist who had served in the German army, joined in November 1919. He was placed in charge of the Party's propaganda and was largely responsible for drafting the 25 Point Programme in 1920 and for renaming the movement the National Socialist German Workers' Party (NSDAP). The following year he supplanted Anton Drexler as party leader and extended National Socialist (Nazi) activities into the media, with the acquisition of the *Munich Observer*, and into paramilitary activism with the formation of the Sturm Abteilung (SA).

The early conception of Nazism was revolutionary. In 1923 Hitler made a bid for power in Munich, clearly encouraged by the success of Mussolini's March on Rome the previous year. The attempt ended in failure; Hitler was tried for treason and sentenced to imprisonment in Landsberg Castle. While he was out of circulation the NSDAP fell into disarray and had to be refounded on his release. Hitler now proceeded to revitalise the party and to alter his whole strategy for achieving power. Instead of coming to power by revolution, he now proposed to achieve his objective by legal means and then to introduce the revolution from above. Between 1925 and 1929 he succeeded in winning over the northern contingents of the NSDAP under Gregor Strasser and Goebbels and in establishing his authority through a series of local party officials known as

Gauleiters. The actual results of these developments are contentious. On the one hand, the NSDAP performed very badly in the Reichstag (or elected chamber) elections, dropping from 32 seats in May 1924 to 14 in December 1924 and 12 in 1928. On the other hand, there is evidence of a major upheaval below the surface within the middle classes which made them more receptive to the appeal of Nazism from 1928 onwards, a process which was accelerated by the Great Depression. The working class, too, became more fragmented and a substantial portion was detached from its normal political allegiance. The electoral impact of such changes was startling. The NSDAP won 107 seats in 1930 and were easily the largest party in the elections of July and November 1932, in which they won 230 and 196 seats respectively.

This increase in support was partly the result of the search by Hitler for respectability and his alliance with the other interests of the right, including the leaders of industrial cartels and the conservative National Party (DNVP). Encouraged by the apparent success of his strategy, Hitler played a double game. Below the surface of German politics the SA terrorised and victimised its opponents. Officially, however, Hitler sought power through election to Germany's highest office, the presidency in March 1932. However, he was defeated by the incumbent, Hindenburg, by 19.4 million votes to 13.4 million. Having failed to enter government through the front door, Hitler became involved in backdoor intrigues, involving the ex-Chancellor, Papen, and the President, Hindenburg. The latter was requested by the current Chancellor, Schleicher, for a dissolution of the Reichstag and the third election within six months. Hindenburg's response, however, was to take the advice of Papen, a political enemy of Schleicher, to appoint Hitler as Chancellor in a coalition cabinet consisting mainly of non-Nazis. Hindenburg and the rest of the conservative right considered that such a course was perfectly safe since Hitler would be effectively controlled. Within days, however, Hitler was to demonstrate that he had a programme of his own.

ANALYSIS (1): WHAT WAS NATIONAL SOCIALISM?

The official name of Hitler's movement throughout the period 1920 to 1945 was the National Socialist German Workers' Party. How accurate was it? Certainly the 25 Point Programme, formulated in 1920, contained principles which could be seen as both nationalist and socialist. The former predominated, demanding 'the union of all Germans in a Greater Germany' (Article 1); the 'revocation of the peace treaties of Versailles and Saint-Germain' (Article 2); the acquisition of 'land and territory to feed our people and settle our surplus population' (Article 3); the replacement of Roman Law by German Law (Article 19); the formation of a people's army (Article 22); and the establishment of 'a strong central state power' (Article 25). The nationalist component was given further emphasis by a strong racial slant. Hence, Jews were to be excluded from German nationhood (Article 4); all 'non-German immigration must be prevented' (Article 8); and non-Germans should be excluded from any influence within the national media (Article 23). The socialist element was apparent mainly in the emphasis on 'physical or mental work' (Article 10); the 'abolition of incomes unearned by work' (Article 11); the 'confiscation of war profits' (Article 12); extensive nationalisation of businesses (Article 13); 'profit-sharing in large industrial enterprises' (Article 14); the extension of old-age insurance (Article 15); and land reform (Article 17).[1]

It soon became clear that Hitler was not particularly committed to the socialist element of the party programme. Indeed, the German Worker's Party was to some extent a misnomer, since he aimed at creating a broadly classless movement which would at the same time appeal to the middle class. The 'creation and maintenance of a healthy middle class' was the purpose of Article 16 and certainly became the basis of Hitler's electoral strategy after 1925. There were Nazis who emphasised the socialist element of their ideology, but these did not include Hitler. In fact some, like the Strassers, came in for serious confrontation with Hitler over the latter's refusal to take socialism seriously. Instead, Hitler focused more and more on racial rather than economic explanations for major historical trends. He argued in his 1925 book *Mein Kampf* (*My Struggle*) that 'The adulteration of the blood and racial deterioration conditioned thereby are the only causes that account for the decline of ancient civilizations; for it is never by war that nations are ruined, but by the loss of their powers of resistance, which are exclusively a characteristic of pure racial blood'.[2]

This raises the key issue concerning the Nazi movement and ideology. Were they unique phenomena dependent on Hitler alone? Or were they part of a more general phenomenon? There is an increasingly important debate between those historians who are Hitler-centric and those who maintain that Nazism was merely a branch of fascism, a general trend which reflected problems throughout the continent during a particular phase of European history. The two main schools have been called 'intentionalists' and 'structuralists'.

Structuralism subsumes a variety of approaches. The longest established is the Marxist view of Nazism as one manifestation of a general crisis of capitalism; East German historians, in particular, maintained that Hitler was above all the tool of big business. Non-Marxist historians acknowledge an economic influence but place this within a broader context of national and international influences. Particular sections of the German population were vulnerable for economic reasons which had their roots in the nineteenth century: the middle classes experienced a crisis of industrialisation which made them susceptible to radical ideas. These, too, had a long history, in the form of pan-Germanism and anti-semitism, and in the quest for *Lebensraum* ('living space'). During the Second Reich (1871–1918) these ideas had been confined to the fringe but, within the crisis of Germany's experience between the Wars, they became the focal point. None of them were new but Nazism was particularly effective, in an eclectic sense, in combining 'snippets of ideas and dogmas of salvation', which could be used as 'a deliberate simplification of political world views'.[3]

Structuralism also emphasises that Nazism was part of the fascist mainstream. The roots were a widespread disillusionment with modernism and rationalism and the emphasis on a curiously twisted form of romanticism. Fascism also emphasised the profound threat of communist and socialist parties while, at the same time, drawing upon a number of socialist ideas which had been modified to appeal to the middle classes. Fascism everywhere was militaristic and expansionist, focusing upon the revival of centralism within the state and future conquest outside it. All fascist parties depended upon the cult of a father-figure and developed mass movements to energise the masses with enthusiasm and commitment. According to Broszat, therefore, National Socialism was rooted in a combination of 'the general European crisis' and 'Germany's national history and its peculiar divergence from the West'.[4]

The 'intentionalists' place more stress on the unique importance of Hitler as the creator of the Nazi programme and ideology: most of his ideas are contained in *Mein Kampf* and the *Zweites Buch* (*Second Book*). Trevor-Roper, for example, emphasises Hitler's own vital influence in the whole process of Nazism: 'about that despot, too, who has often been represented as a tool, but whose personal power was in fact so undisputed that he rode to the end above the chaos he had created, and concealed its true nature.'[5] Bullock, too, accentuates the personal influence of the leader (*Führer*).[6] Erdmann goes further: 'Hitler's greatness was diabolical: it was that of a world figure who confused the minds of men.'[7] A vital component of Nazism was the 'Führer principle' (*Führerprinzip*). It is true that the cult of leadership is to be found in all fascist movements, but it was of particular importance in the Nazi context since Hitler's ideas were crucial in defining the nature of Nazi eclecticism. Fascism without Mussolini is just about imaginable, and historians have even drawn a distinction between 'Mussolinianism' and fascism. But no one has seriously suggested separating 'Hitlerism' from Nazism. Above all, Hitler provided Nazism with a unique vision of racial purity and anti-semitism which were entirely absent in Italy. In this respect, as in others, the generic label of German fascism hardly seems appropriate.

Which is the more realistic approach? There are certain obvious deficiencies in structuralism. The Marxist approach to Nazism as capitalism in crisis does not explain why some countries remained democracies in spite of experiencing similar problems. Capitalism, in other words, was equally capable of assuming democratic forms. On the other hand, we should not write out structuralism. The popularity of Hitler is impossible to explain without the existence of a strong degree of receptivity within Germany – and this could well be set in a wider European context. There was much in Hitler which was ludicrous: it was converted into a compelling form of radicalism because it worked upon the needs of the population at the time. Structuralism is essential to explain the extent of this appeal but cannot cover the way in which the attraction was presented. This was very much within the scope of intentionalism.

Questions

1. Was 'National Socialism' the right name for Hitler's movement?
2. Were the Nazis fascist?

ANALYSIS (2): WHY DID HITLER COME TO POWER IN 1933?

Hitler was appointed Chancellor by President Hindenburg on 30 January 1933. He was the leader of the largest party in the Reichstag and also had the support of much of the conservative right who had dominated Germany politically since 1929. The explanation as to why this happened can be advanced in three stages. First, Nazism was fortunate in that the Weimar Republic (formed in 1919 and ended in 1933) had become a flawed structure which contained a destabilised and increasingly volatile population. Second, Nazism emerged as a dynamic movement which was capable of gaining support from a substantial part of the disillusioned electorate. And third, the conservative right provided a channel which enabled the new dynamic to penetrate and force open the flawed structure.

The rise of Hitler depended directly on the vulnerability of the Weimar Republic. Although in many respects an advanced democracy, the Republic was politically flawed and susceptible to economic crisis.[8] There were practical difficulties arising out of the constitution. Proportional representation, without a threshold, produced a multiplicity of parties, encouraged splinter groups and made coalition governments inevitable, with all the potential for internal disagreement which these so often carry. This was exacerbated at certain points in the history of the Republic by economic crises, especially those of 1921–3 and 1929–31. The collapse of democracy in 1929 was due to the interaction of the two processes. The Great Coalition – which comprised the Social Democratic Party (SPD), the Centre, the People's Party (DVP) and the Democratic Party (DDP) – was already in disarray before 1929 but was brought down by the disagreement between the SPD and the Centre over proposals to cut unemployment benefit. The results were the decline of party politics and the growth of authoritarian government with less and less recourse to the Reichstag. As will be seen, this was an ideal situation for the Nazi Party. The crisis of the democratic Republic saw the alienation of substantial numbers of the German people.

The radical left became bitter opponents because of the Government's ruthless suppression of the 1919 revolt of the Spartacus League, the incipient Communist Party. The result was that the Communists could at no stage be relied upon to support the SPD against any offensive from the conservative right. The latter became increasingly likely with the triumph of the 'stab in the back' myth. This claim that republican politicians cravenly surrendered to the Allies in November 1918 – against the wish of the German army – was started by Hindenburg in 1919 and combined with criticism of the Treaty of Versailles in a devastating attack on the whole rationale of the Republic. Between the two political extremes lay the supporters of the moderate liberal parties (the DVP and the DDP) and the SPD. But substantial numbers of these eventually abandoned their normal party allegiances because of the impact of economic crisis and the apparent inability of the coalitions to deal with it.

The Nazi Party fully exploited these flaws and this disillusionment. The early dynamic of Nazism, it is true, had very limited appeal. This was because it was a small fringe movement seeking power through revolution. In 1923 Hitler attempted to seize power in Bavaria through the Munich Putsch as a prelude to marching on Berlin: this ended in complete failure. But the new dynamic, developed by Hitler between 1924 and 1926, was far more effective in taking advantage of the problems of the Republic. The intention was to seek power through the constitutional process while, in the longer term, resorting to revolutionary change: revolution would follow power rather than achieve it. This was more likely to appeal to an electorate who were on the point of abandoning traditional loyalties without wanting to go through the experience of a revolution. Hitler was able to appeal directly to each class and sector within this electorate by making specific pledges calculated to it individually. At the same time, he used several more general policies as a means of cutting through class differences: these were based on a nationalist offensive against the 'stab in the back' and Versailles, a *völkisch* emphasis on the need for German expansion through *Lebensraum*, and the identification of 'race enemies' like the Jews. This dual approach to party policy meant that the NSDAP became the only party in the Weimar Republic able to project an appeal to all sectors of the population. In the words of T. Childers, the Nazis could speak 'the language of both transcendent class or even national solidarity and sectarian special interest'.[9] The process was carried out, especially after 1928, by an effective propaganda machine, organised by Goebbels and delivered by a style of oratory which singled Hitler out from the more staid politicians of Weimar. Hitler was therefore able to convert negatives into positives, to turn resentment against the Republic into support for the Nazi movement.

Where did this come from? A considerable amount of research has been carried out on the defection to the NSDAP during the late 1920s and early 1930s. The initial tendency was to see Nazism as having an appeal primarily to the middle classes, with minority additions from the working class and from the upper levels of society – neither of whom were as volatile in transferring their political allegiance. The overall emphasis of this has now been modified in favour of a more widespread support for Hitler.

It is still possible to say that the middle classes made up the largest single proportion of Nazi support, and that their defection from their traditional parties was vitally important in converting Nazism into a mass movement. Initially they had voted in large numbers for the DDP and the DVP, although some also supported the DNVP and, if they were Catholic, the Centre. Some historians, like Childers, have argued that the basis for the middle-class movement towards the NSDAP had been established during the late 1920s, even before the onset of Depression from 1929.[10] Others maintain that the flow occurred only after 1929, making it a direct result of the Great Depression. The middle classes found unbearable the impact of a second economic crisis destroying the apparent recovery from the first. The psychological blow was so profound that they made an uncharacteristic move away from the moderate centre to the radical fringe. It is, of course, possible to synthesise the two approaches. The older section of the middle class, comprising artisans, small retailers and peasant farmers, formed the core of the middle-class support for Hitler and were throwing their support behind him before the Depression. Theirs was a disillusionment with the structure and policies of the Republic itself. To these was added the weight of much of the new middle class – non-manual employees, civil servants and teachers – who aligned themselves with Nazism as a result of the Depression. It is possible that they were moving in this direction anyway.

But the simple fact is that the NSDAP secured only 12 seats in the Reichstag election of 1928; it therefore took the Depression to convert a trickle of middle-class support into a flood.

There is a deeper controversy over the connection between Nazism and the working class. It was once strongly argued that the working class remained largely loyal to the parties of the left which, in any case, had a distinctively proletarian appeal. The Communist Party (KPD) was especially class-based and its support actually increased during the Reichstag elections of 1930 and 1932. Although the SPD lost seats, it came nowhere near the collapse suffered by the parties of the centre, clearly indicating that it retained the bulk of its support. The proletariat, by this analysis, was less drawn to Nazism because, in the words of P. D. Stachura, 'The Party was unable to establish a significant working-class constituency because it did not develop a coherent interpretation of "German Socialism".' This was partly because Hitler's 'innate contempt and distrust of the proletariat remained paramount'.[11] Other historians, such as Muhlberger, are not convinced by the 'middle-class thesis' of Nazism.[12] Recent research has tended to support the view that working-class input was substantial. Studies of Nazi membership records show something like 40 per cent of the membership coming from the working class, while 60 per cent of the SA were of the same origins. Parallel research on electoral trends has, through computer analysis of statistical data, produced very similar voting results. According to Fischer, 'a good 40 per cent of the NSDAP's voters were working class, remarkably similar to the proportion of workers in the party itself'.[13] The likely synthesis here is that the working class never came to provide the largest body of support for Nazism. In that respect, the original views seem correct. On the other hand, it is possible to overestimate the continued loyalty of the working class to the parties of the left. After 1928 substantial shifts did occur: the growth of the Communists was more than offset by the decline of the SPD. The latter shrank by between a quarter and a third: many of these lost votes almost certainly went straight to the Nazis. Thus, although the NSDAP was not primarily a working-class party and the majority of workers remained with the parties of the left, the inflow of working-class support for Nazism was still a vital factor in the conversion of Nazism into a mass movement.

The attitudes of the upper classes to Nazism were largely pragmatic. Landowners, businessmen and industrialists saw in Hitler the prospects of safety from the threat of communism and socialism on the left. Arguably, they saw beyond this and looked to Nazism to deliver over to them a disciplined and constrained workforce. They looked to Hitler to undo the pro-trade-union and welfare policies of most of the governments of the Weimar Republic. Even those who distrusted the violence and vulgarities of the Nazi movement were still likely to be supporting it indirectly. It was unlikely that the affluent levels of German society after 1929 voted in significant numbers for any party to the left of the DNVP, and the DNVP itself was in close collaboration with the NSDAP after Hugenberg assumed the leadership. Hence the Nazis benefited considerably from the respectability, publicity and, of course, funding brought by a relatively narrow but highly influential sector of society.

After 1928, therefore, Hitler succeeded in collecting for the NSDAP much of the electorate which had become disillusioned with the Republic's manifest deficiencies. This was essential for Hitler's rise to prominence but it does not fully explain his rise to power. A further step was needed – a means of forcing a way in through the Republic's fissures. This was greatly assisted by the drift to authoritarian rule after 1929 in which the democracy of the Republic was systematically undermined by the conservative right. The first stage was the recruitment of Brüning to form a government based on the Centre Party; lacking a majority in the Reichstag he came increasingly to depend on the use of Article 48 of the Constitution which made possible legislation by presidential decree. In 1932 Papen and Schleicher abandoned any remaining pretence of relating the chancellorship to a party base in the Reichstag and made executive decrees the normal legislative process. Hence by 1933 the ground had been well prepared for the emergence of dictatorship.

But why were the conservative right willing to allow Hitler and the radical right to benefit from this? The explanation seems to be that the conservative right (which included the DNVP, some of the army command, President Hindenburg and Chancellors Papen and Schleicher) intended to use Nazism for their own purpose. They believed that the Republic had outlived its usefulness and that any return to the party politics of the 1920s was impossible. Instead, conservative constitutional theorists argued in *Unsere Partei* that the party system would eventually fracture and be replaced by a broad front. For this reason, the DNVP therefore aimed to create a broad 'movement' of the right which would also include the NSDAP. The latter could, in fact, be used for its radical impetus. It had the capacity to destroy the Republic, but once that was achieved it would be brought into line with the more conservative objectives of the DNVP. The collaboration between the Nazis and the DNVP was crucial; Hiden goes so far as to say that it 'played handmaiden to Adolf Hitler and his movement at the close of the 1920s'.[14]

This strategy, which eventually proved to be fatally flawed, provided Hitler with access to power. His appointment as Chancellor was due to a fortuitous circumstance – the personal rivalry between the last two Chancellors, Papen and Schleicher. The latter faced a political crisis when, in January 1933, the Reichstag challenged his use of Article 48. The Constitution provided a loophole in that the President could dissolve the Reichstag and call an election. But, having already done this twice in 1932, Hindenburg preferred to find an alternative Chancellor. This explains his receptiveness to Papen's recommendation that Hitler should be appointed, with himself given a watching brief as Vice-Chancellor.

Hence Hitler came to power largely through a conspiracy. Yet this does not mean that the Nazis did little themselves to achieve it. The conservative right would not have been so willing to collaborate with a weak fringe group. It was evident to them that the NSDAP had managed more effectively than any other party to mobilise popular discontent against the Republic. Hitler appeared to them an elemental force which they intended to use in their own way. And they thought they *could*.

Questions

1. Were Hitler's aims 'revolutionary'?
2. Was the NSDAP a 'classless' party?
3. Was Hitler given power?

SOURCES

1. THE IDEOLOGY AND PROGRAMME OF NAZISM

Source A: from the Programme of the German Workers' Party, February 1920.

1. We demand the union of all Germans, on the basis of the right of the self-determination of peoples, to form a Great Germany.
2. We demand equality of rights for the German people in its dealings with other nations, and abolition of the Peace Treaties of Versailles and Saint-Germain.
3. We demand land and territory (colonies) for the nourishment of our people and for settling our surplus population.
4. None but members of the nation may be citizens of the State. None but those of German blood, whatever their creed, may be members of the nation. No Jew, therefore, may be a member of the nation. . . .
7. We demand that the State shall make it its first duty to promote the industry and livelihood of the citizens of the State . . .
8. All further non-German immigration must be prevented . . .
11. [We demand] abolition of incomes unearned by work. . . .
13. We demand the nationalization of all businesses which have been amalgamated.
14. We demand that there shall be profit-sharing in the great industries.
15. We demand a general development of provision for old age.
16. We demand the creation and maintenance of a healthy middle class . . .
17. We demand a land reform suitable to our national requirements . . .
25. That all the foregoing requirements may be realized we demand the creation of a strong central power of the Reich . . .

Source B: from a speech by Hitler on 13 April 1923.

It has ever been the right of the stronger, before God and man, to see his will prevail. History proves that he who lacks strength is not served in the slightest by 'pure law' . . . All of nature is one great struggle between strength and weakness, an eternal victory of the strong over the weak. If it were any different, nature would be in a state of putrefaction. The nation which would violate this elementary law would rot away.

Source C: from Hitler's *Mein Kampf*.

The art of all truly great national leaders has at all times primarily consisted of this: not to divide the attention of a people, but to concentrate that attention on a single enemy. The more unified the fighting spirit of a nation, the greater the magnetic attraction of a movement, the more forceful the power of its thrust. It is part of the genius of a great leader to make it appear as though even the most distant enemies belonged in the same category; for weak and fickle characters, if faced by many different enemies, will easily begin to have doubts about the justness of their cause.

Source D: Otto Strasser's recollection of a conversation with Hitler (published in 1940).

I remember one of my first conversations with him. It was nearly our first quarrel.

'Power!' screamed Adolf. 'We must have power!' 'Before we gain it,' I replied firmly, 'let us decide what we propose to do with it. Our programme is too vague; we must construct something solid and enduring.'

Hitler, who even then could hardly bear contradiction, thumped the table and barked: 'Power first! Afterwards we can act as circumstances dictate!'

Source E: from a speech by Hitler at an election meeting in March 1928.

We can conclude that bourgeois nationalism has failed, and that the concept of Marxist socialism has made life impossible in the long run. These old lines of confrontation must be eradicated along with the old parties, because they are barring the nation's path into the future. We are eradicating them by releasing the two concepts of nationalism and socialism and harnessing them for a new goal, towards which we are working, full of hope, for the highest form of socialism is burning devotion to the nation.

Source F: Otto Strasser's record of a discussion with Hitler on the subject of socialism in 1930 (published in 1940).

Strasser: All that is very simple for you, Herr Hitler, but it only serves to emphasize the profound difference in our revolutionary and Socialist ideas ... The real reason is that you want to strangle the social revolution for the sake of legality and your new collaboration with the bourgeois parties of the Right. *Hitler*: I am a Socialist, and a very different kind of Socialist ... your kind of Socialism is nothing but Marxism. The mass of the working classes want nothing but bread and games. They will never understand the meaning of an ideal, and we cannot hope to win them over to one. What we have to do is to select from a new master-class men who will not allow themselves to be guided, like you, by the morality of pity. Those who rule must know that they have the right to rule because they belong to a superior race.

Questions

Figures in square brackets after questions indicate possible allocation of marks by examiners.

1. (i) What general term is normally used to describe the concept of struggle contained in Source B? [1]
    (ii) Explain Strasser's reference to 'your new collaboration with the bourgeois parties of the Right' (Source F). [2]
2. How much evidence is there in Source A that the Nazis intended to follow a policy based on nationalism? [4]
*3. How valuable are Sources D and F to the historian studying Nazi ideology? [5]
4. Using Sources A, D and F, explain the different viewpoints of Hitler and Strasser concerning the implementation of socialism. [5]
5. Using Sources A to F and your own knowledge, discuss the view that National Socialism before 1933 was 'pragmatic rather than ideological'. [8]

Worked answer

*3. [The answer to this question should be confined to one – possibly two – carefully argued paragraphs. If at all possible, two sides should be presented, although these need not be evenly balanced. There is also scope for the inclusion of additional material, provided this is carefully controlled and directly relevant to the question.]

Sources D and F provide the historian with a valuable insight into Hitler's political thinking. Source D shows that he could be strongly pragmatic: his emphasis on 'Power first!' and on acting as 'circumstances dictate' confirms his change of political strategy after the failure of the Munich Putsch in 1923. Strasser amplifies this in Source F with his references to Hitler's policy of 'legality' and 'collaboration' with the right. Source F also reveals the extent of the ideological split within the Nazi Party between Hitler's interpretation of socialism and Strasser's. Source D also provides an intriguing picture of the more impetuous side of Hitler, who 'screamed' and 'thumped the table and barked'.

There are two drawbacks of which the historian needs to be aware. The first is that Otto Strasser had every reason to give a distorted picture of Hitler's views and mannerisms. He left Germany under a cloud and wrote his accounts while in exile. Second, the impressions were actually published in 1940, over a decade after the incidents: this opens up the possibility of inaccuracy in the precise wording. He was also concerned to present himself in a positive way by using phrases such as 'I replied firmly' (Source D). But these disadvantages are offset by the rarity of a frank, if hostile, view of Hitler from a Nazi colleague.

SOURCES

2. THE BASE OF HITLER'S SUPPORT BEFORE 1933

Source G: Reichstag election results 1928–32 (number of seats).

	1928	*1930*	*1932* (1)	*1932* (2)
NSDAP	12	107	230	196
DNVP	73	41	37	52
DVP	45	30	7	11
Z	62	68	75	70
DDP	25	20	4	2
SPD	153	143	133	121
KPD	54	77	89	100

Source H: the social origins of members of the SA between 1925 and 1933.

Class	*Occupational group*	*% of SA*
Working	Agricultural	2.9
	Unskilled	15.4
	Skilled	35.4
	Public sector	0.9
	Apprentices	1.5
	Servants	0.4
	Subtotal	56.5
Lower middle and middle	Master artisans	1.3
	Non-grad. professions	3.3
	Salaried staff	8.8

	Civil servants	2.7
	Soldiers and NCOs	0.0
	Salesmen	10.4
	Farmers	4.3
	Family helpers	2.1
	Subtotal	32.9
Upper middle and upper	Senior salaried staff	0.2
	Senior civil servants	0.1
	Military officers	0.0
	University students	4.1
	Graduate professions	1.2
	Entrepreneurs	0.2
	Subtotal	5.8

Source I: the social composition of the part of the electorate voting for the NSDAP (%).

	1928	*1930*	*1932 (1)*	*1932 (2)*
Working class	40	40	39	39
Middle and upper middle class	59	60	61	60
% of total vote going to NSDAP	2	15	31	27

Source J: a confidential analysis, prepared by the KPD of the rise in support for the NSDAP (1931).

National Fascism [the NSDAP] is the opposite side of the coin from Social Fascism [the SPD]. The betrayal of socialism, of the German working people and thereby of the German nation by the SPD's leaders has led millions of workers, rural workers and impoverished members of the middle classes into the ranks of the NSDAP. In particular the disciplined, militarily-trained storm sections of the NSDAP – the SS and the SA – boast a high percentage of industrial workers and in particular unemployed proletarians.

Source K: from the application form of a recruit to the SA.

. . . I completed my three-year apprenticeship as an electrical fitter at the firm of Karl Diehl. I was politically active in the Iron Front paramilitary for about one and a half years. After I had gradually become aware of the SPD's poor leadership and that its efforts couldn't help us, I resigned from the organisation. On the other hand, I am convinced that the new Germany, led by our People's Chancellor Adolf Hitler, signifies recovery and resurgence and I wish to devote all my efforts to this.

Questions

1. Explain briefly:
   (i) the absence within the SA of 'soldiers and NCOs' and 'military officers' (Source H). [1]
   (ii) the 'Iron Front' (Source K). [2]
2. To what extent is it possible to detect from Source G alone the origins of the increased Nazi electoral support in 1930 and 1932? [5]
3. Assess the contrasting value to the historian of the evidence provided in Sources J and K. [5]
*4. 'The rise of Nazism between 1928 and 1932 was based on the support of the middle classes.' To what extent do Sources G to I show this? [7]
5. In addition to Sources G to K, what other types of source would be useful to the historian studying the increase in support for the Nazis between 1928 and 1932? [5]

Worked answer

*4. [The quotation is obviously too one-sided and needs to be rebalanced. It is therefore important to present a clear overall argument. The first sentence or two might contain a basic interpretation which can then be supported by more detailed reference to the sources. The concluding sentences might suggest something a little more subtle – if there is time.]

This statement is only partly correct. In terms of electoral support, the middle and upper middle classes seem to predominate. Source I quantifies them at between 60 and 61 per cent of Nazi voters. This kept pace with the increase in the total vote for the Nazis (15 per cent in 1930 and 31 per cent in June 1932), which was accomplished partly through the declining support for the three parties for which the middle classes usually voted – the DNVP, DVP and DDP: Source G shows these down in June 1932 to 37, 7 and 4 seats respectively. It does, therefore, seem that the NSDAP built the core of its support from the remains of the middle-class parties.

On the other hand, this would not have been enough to create a mass movement. This could be achieved only by attracting a substantial part of the working class. After all, as Source G shows, the name of the party, NSDAP, still contained the word *Arbeiter* (workers). Hence the 39 per cent and 40 per cent of Nazi voters drawn from the working class (Source I) were crucial in explaining why the NSDAP was able to overtake the SPD in June 1932 (Source G) as Germany's largest party. The quotation also underestimates the importance of the working class in providing members of activist movements like the SA, as opposed to more passive electoral support. Source H shows that 56.5 per cent of the SA were recruited from this part of society.

Overall, these sources show that the NSDAP drew most of their vote from the middle classes and became the largest party attracting the middle classes. They also drew substantial support from the working classes but were unable to displace either the SPD or KPD to become the main party of the working class. They did, however, manage to combine their middle-class core and additions from the working class to become the only party in Germany to cut through class barriers.

2

THE ESTABLISHMENT OF DICTATORSHIP

BACKGROUND NARRATIVE

Within days of his appointment as Chancellor, on 30 January 1933, Hitler requested a dissolution of the Reichstag so that he could increase the number of seats for the NSDAP. During the election campaign he made use of emergency decrees, issued under Article 48 of the Constitution, to hamstring the other parties, especially the SPD and KPD; the reason given for this was the Reichstag fire, which was blamed on the Communists. Although the NSDAP did not achieve an overall majority in the election, they did succeed in increasing the number of their seats from 196 to 288.

The next objective was to change the Constitution. Because of an entrenched clause this required a two-thirds majority. In March 1933 Hitler achieved this through two measures. One was the banning of the KPD deputies from assuming their seats because of their alleged implication in the Reichstag fire. The other was a deal struck up with the Centre Party guaranteeing Catholic liberties in exchange for the absence of any opposition from the Centre party to Hitler's measures. As a result Hitler was able to secure the passage of the Enabling Act which allowed the Chancellor as well as the Reichstag to issue legislation. This measure was used to extend Hitler's already considerable powers. In April 1933 the Chancellor decreed that the local state legislatures (*Landtage*) need not be consulted by the local state officials in issuing legislation, while in 1934 the *Landtage* were abolished altogether. Measures were then taken against potential opponents. In May 1940 the trade union movement was to be replaced by the Nazi-organised German Labour Front (DAF) and, in June, the Reichstag was effectively cleared out by the banning of all political parties other than the NSDAP. Also in 1934 Hitler took two measures to consolidate his power. The first was the elimination of the SA leadership in the Night of the Long Knives (30 June), the second the combination of the positions of Chancellor and President into the title of Führer (August).

These changes have long been considered part of an overall 'legal revolution', a term which has caused considerable controversy. The two interpretations in this section deal with two related issues. First, how 'legal' were the changes made? Second, how effective were they?

ANALYSIS (1): HOW 'LEGAL' WAS THE POLITICAL REVOLUTION BETWEEN 1933 AND 1934?

Hitler's actions between 1933 and 1934 were ordered so as to convert a regime which he detested into one which would enable the transmission of Nazi values to the German people. At the same time, his options for change were limited by the initial constraints under which he operated. He had, for example, been appointed head of a cabinet in which there were only three Nazis: the view of Papen was that 'we have roped him'. He was also subject to the ultimate authority of President Hindenburg, who remained commander-in-chief of the armed forces. In such a situation any change by Hitler had to be gradual to avoid giving reason for his dismissal by the President or his overthrow by the army. This underlies the notion of 'legal revolution'.

There is much to support the use of this term as a description of Hitler's overall approach in the opening years of his regime. He had already followed a strategy of legality after the failure of the Munich Putsch in 1923, achieving power constitutionally with the intention of subsequently introducing a 'revolution from above'. This 'revolution' was now accomplished, step by step, within the literal terms of the Constitution of the Weimar Republic.

There are several examples of this process. The Enabling Act, passed on 24 March, contained as part of its preamble the words 'The requirements of legal Constitutional change having been met'.[1] This was a clear reference to the achievement of the two-thirds majority required within the Reichstag for such an important amendment. The Enabling Act, in turn, became the vehicle by which the Chancellor used executive powers to modify the whole range of political functions within the Reich. The bureaucracy was brought into line with the new relationship between executive and legislature by the law of 7 April 'for the restoration of the professional civil service' which purged the bureaucracy of potential opponents and non-Aryans. The system of state government was reorganised by the law of 31 March 'for the Co-ordination of the *Länder* of the Reich'. The whole concept of *Gleichschaltung* (co-ordination) was therefore slipped through with at least a pretence at a legal basis. The NSDAP were given the monopoly of political power through the law against the new formation of parties, passed on 14 July 1933. Finally, the Chancellorship and the Presidency were combined on 1 August 1934, following the death of President Hindenburg.

At first sight the extent of the constitutional changes introduced scarcely warrant the description 'revolution', especially by contrast with the changes brought by the Bolsheviks to Russia. After all, the Reichstag and the Reichsrat remained intact as legislative institutions, the former elected, the latter appointed by the *Länder*. Lenin had, by contrast, taken the decision to remove any remaining connection with western-style constitutent assemblies and to substitute a legislative system based upon soviets. In Germany all of the previous ministries were retained. Indeed, the lists of official positions within Hitler's cabinet were remarkably similar to those within the Weimar Republic: these included the Foreign Minister, Interior Minister, Finance Minister, and Ministers for Economics, Justice, Defence, Food, Posts, Labour and Transport. By this analysis the nazification of the institutions of the Weimar Republic occurred in such a way as to minimise the chance of a sudden break which might generate resistance. The process was done step by step, each depending on the one before. There was therefore a certain inexorable logic.

From another viewpoint, the concept of 'legal revolution' is paradoxical at the best of times. When applied to the development of Nazi dictatorship the paradox becomes perverse. The whole emphasis was on using the legal powers of the Weimar Constitution to destroy its political authority, not to amend it. Throughout the period there was at best a very thinly disguised use of legality and, at worst, a blatant disregard for it.

The observance of the constitution was strictly limited: the letter of the law may have been kept, but the spirit of the law was not. Hitler's objective was nothing less than the destruction of the Weimar Republic, which he achieved on three counts. First, he converted emergency powers from a precautionary to a regular process. The Enabling Act turned Article 48 on its head by making permanent what had originally been conceived as a temporary power. This completely destroyed the original aim. Article 48 had been included to preserve democracy against future enemies, whereas the Enabling Act was clearly based on the premise that democracy itself was the enemy. A second principle to be shredded was the autonomous rights of the *Länder*. Laws issued under the Enabling Act abolished the powers of the *Länder* legislatures and subordinated the state Ministers President to the Ministry of the Interior in Berlin. This destroyed the entire federal system which had been a crucial part of the Weimar Constitution. Third, the Law against the New Formation of Parties wiped out the multi-party system, a vital ingredient of the Weimar Republic. Without the element of choice the purpose of voting was nullified and with it the extension of the franchise to men and women over twenty. Proportional representation, too, ceased to have any meaning. The notion of legality was therefore a mockery. A democratic constitution was imploded by anti-democrats who targeted its emergency changes inwards.

It is not even certain that the Nazis observed the letter of the Constitution. Hitler's 'legal' changes were accompanied by a considerable degree of mobilised pressure – of the very type that the Constitution was originally conceived to prevent. Article 48 was intended for Presidential use to put down mass activism, not to unleash it against selected constitutional targets. Hildebrand refers to 'Nazi terrorist tactics' and maintains that 'it was often difficult to distinguish terroristic from legal measures'.[2] For example, the Nazi control over the Ministry of the Interior and other key organs of State gave them control over the police apparatus. Goering used this to create an auxiliary police force, the Gestapo, which comprised members of both the SA and the SS. The result was paradoxical: a rampage of law and order directed against political enemies of the Nazi movement – in other words, an officially sanctioned continuation of previously illegal methods. The same involvement of the violent men of the SA can be seen in the intimidation of Social Democrat deputies during the Reichstag vote on the Enabling Bill in March 1933. By the whole range of legal principles, from constitutional law to natural equity, such a gross interference would normally be seen to have invalidated the outcome.

The Nazi revolution included also the element of the mass movement which was entirely incompatible with the principle of legality. This was apparent even during the course of the so-called period of legality, especially in the town hall revolutions, by which the SA purged local governments, and by the boycotting of Jewish shops from 1 April 1933. It might, of course, be argued that the real revolutionaries were the leaders of the SA and that Hitler took emergency measures against these in the Night of the Long Knives. On the other hand, Hitler stayed the second revolution not through a preference for legality, but rather for reasons of safety. If he was to remain in power Hitler had to avoid the possibility of a military coup launched by conservatives, something which might be triggered by premature expressions of radicalism. Thus caution had more to do with common sense and pragmatism than with legality – which, in any case, can hardly be used to describe the method by which the leaders of the SA were disposed of.

Finally, the Nazi apparatus came to be dominated by a body which was as far from the constitutional apparatus of the Weimar Republic as it is possible to conceive. The SS/Gestapo/SD complex came to dominate the whole regime. According to Schoenbaum, 'in one form or another the SS made foreign policy, military policy and agricultural policy. It administered occupied territories as a kind of self-contained Ministry of the Interior and maintained itself economically with autonomous enterprises.' This was a revolution in the political structure of Germany which transcended all notions of legality.

Questions

1. Why did Hitler stress the importance of 'legality' in the Nazi revolution?
2. Was the 'legal revolution' anything more than the artificial contrivance of Nazi propaganda?

ANALYSIS (2): HOW EFFECTIVE WAS THE NAZI POLITICAL REVOLUTION?

This question can be approached in two ways. In the first place, analysis can focus on the extent to which the Nazi regime effectively differed institutionally from its predecessors. This has been largely dealt with in Analysis (1). Second, how efficiently were the changes introduced and subsequently implemented? This will be the focus here.

The nazification of the whole system of government in Germany has traditionally led to the view that organisation was tight and carefully structured. The precision with which the Nazi legal revolution occurred also suggests Hitler's full control over the whole process. The Third Reich, in other words, was a model of efficiency precisely because the effort taken to establish it had been so minimal. This whole approach is, however, open to fundamental question and a number of revisionist historians have presented a very different picture. It is now argued that, far from being orderly, the Nazi dictatorship was actually prone to internal conflict which resulted in a surprising degree of chaos. The basic problem was that the Third Reich was a hotchpotch of over-lapping institutions and structures. This was the result of the minimalist approach to constitutional change. Instead of knocking down the old structure, the Nazis had simply constructed another on top of it. The effect was the duplication of functions and the conflict between officials in central and local government. Examples abound of the over-lapping of traditional and new institutions creating a web of conflicting structures.

At the centre the process was especially pronounced. Special Deputies were appointed in parallel to the heads of the old government ministries, often performing similar functions to them. For example, the General Inspector for German Roads, a newly appointed official, overlapped some of the functions of the traditional Minister for Posts and Transport: the result was frequent conflict between the respective incumbents, Todt and von Rubenach. The Youth Leader of the Reich, von Schirach, similarly duplicated the functions of the Minister of Education, Ley. The confusion was compounded by the development of a third layer of personnel, who were outside the scope both of the normal ministries and of the parallel party functionaries. These included the office of the Deputy Führer, the Four Year Plan Office (along, confusingly, with its six ministries), and the SS/Gestapo/SD complex under the authority of Himmler. All this resulted in widespread ineffici-ency. The main problems were the duplication of functions between agencies and growing conflict between officials. On numerous occa-sions appeals were made to the Führer himself to arbitrate in disputes between them. His reponse was to distance himself from routine disputes and to rely upon Hess as a mediator. Faced with this sort of problem, it is hardly surprising that there was a threat of creeping inertia among subordinates as officials at all levels shied away from taking responsibility through fear of making a mistake – not of policy but of jurisdiction.

Much the same problems applied in the area of local government. Each of the *Länder* retained its traditional official, the Minister President, or Prime Minister. After the legislation of 1934 had ended the autonomous powers of the state legislatures, the Minister President became the local official subordinate to the Ministry of the Interior. This would seem a logical enough process: the consolidation of Hitler's dictatorship through the process of centralisation. But the whole thing became more cumbersome with the addition of ten Reich governors, appointed by the regime from the most important of the Party Gauleiters. Again, their function was to ensure the full implementation of the Führer's policy, but again they came into conflict with existing officials. Overall, Noakes and Pridham argue, the state authorities were a façade, 'the substance of which was progressively being eaten away by the cancerous growth of the new organization under individuals appointed by Hitler'.[3]

Explaining this complex process has produced a major historiographical debate. There are two broad possibilities. One is that Hitler did all this on purpose. The 'intentionalists' argue that Hitler deliberately set his institutions and officials against each other in order to maintain his own position as the only one who could manoeuvre between them. Bracher, for example, maintains that Hitler remained detached from the struggles between officials: 'the antagonisms of power were only resolved in the the key position of the omnipotent Führer'; indeed 'the dictator held a key position precisely because of the confusion of conflicting power groups'.[4] Similarly, Hildebrand believes that 'The confusion of functions among a multitude of mutually hostile authorities made it necessary and possible for the Führer to take decisions in every case of dispute, and can be regarded as a foundation of his power'.[5]

In contrast to this, other historians, usually categorised as 'structuralists' or 'functionalists', stress that the chaos was entirely unintended, the byproduct of confusion and neglect. Far from being able to distance himself effectively from competing officials in order to maintain his position, Hitler simply showed incompetence and hence administrative weakness. According to Broszat: 'The authoritative Führer's will was expressed only irregularly, unsystematically and incoherently'.[6] Mommsen maintains that 'Instead of functioning as a balancing element in the government, Hitler disrupted the conduct of affairs by continually acting on sudden impulses, each one different, and partly by delaying decisions on current matters'.[7]

Which of these is the more likely scenario? As is often the case in historical interpretation, a judicious combination of the two schools is possible. There is no doubt that Hitler did whatever he could to fragment potential opposition: indeed, he had already welcomed the partial collapse of the party while he was in Landsberg prison. It is not, therefore, beyond the realms of possibility that he welcomed discordance within the State in order to regulate his subordinates and prevent the emergence of 'overmighty' barons. The 'intentionalists' therefore have a point. On the other hand, it is difficult to imagine this being planned. The deliberate projection of chaos carries enormous risks which may seem justifiable in retrospect but which can hardly have been chanced at the time. In any case, if the original 'legal revolution' had been 'planned' on the basis of the simplest and most direct route to dictatorship, what would have been the logic in complicating the process by deliberately creating overlapping bureaucratic layers? The balance of credibility therefore switches here to the 'structuralists'.

But only when considering the origins of the chaos. Once we focus on its continuation, Bracher's perspective makes more sense. Conceding that the chaos was unintended, what possible motive could Hitler have had for tolerating it unless it was in his interests to do so? Would it be too much to assume that, having adjusted his approach to taking power by 1933 and to consolidating it by 1934, Hitler would have been unable to correct any aberrations thrown up in the process? It is more likely that it suited Hitler to live with the chaos which had emerged despite his efforts because this was an effective way of cancelling out trouble-makers within the party. Broszat therefore convincingly explains the origins of the Nazi administrative chaos, with Bracher providing the vital reason for its perpetuation.

Questions

1. In administrative terms, did the Weimar Republic ever give way completely to the Third Reich?
2. Does the notion of 'ordered chaos' make any sense when applied to the political system of Nazi Germany?

SOURCES

1. THE LEGAL REVOLUTION

Source A: an extract from the Constitution of the Weimar Republic, 11 August 1919.

ARTICLE 48. In the event that the public order and security are seriously disturbed or endangered, the Reich President may take the measures necessary for their restoration, intervening, if necessary, with the aid of the armed forces. For this purpose he may abrogate temporarily, wholly or in part, the fundamental principles laid down in Articles 114, 115, 117, 118, 123, 124 and 153.

The Reich President must, without delay, inform the Reichstag of all measures taken under . . . this Article. These measures may be rescinded on demand of the Reichstag.

ARTICLE 76. The Constitution may be amended by law, but acts . . . amending the Constitution can take effect only if two-thirds of the legal number of members are present and at least two-thirds of those present consent.

Source B: from the Law for Terminating the Suffering of the People and Nation, 24 March 1933.

The Reichstag has passed the following law, which has been approved by the Reichsrat. The requirements of legal Constitutional change having been met, it is being proclaimed herewith.

ARTICLE 1. In addition to the procedure outlined for the passage of legislation in the Constitution, the government also is authorized to pass laws . . .

ARTICLE 2. Laws passed by the government may deviate from the Constitution, provided they do not deal with the institutions, as such, of Reichstag and Reichsrat. The prerogatives of the President remain unchanged.

ARTICLE 3. The laws passed by the government shall be issued by the Chancellor and published in the official gazette . . .

Source C: the Law Against the New Formation of Parties, 14 July 1933.

The government has passed the following law, which is being proclaimed herewith:

ARTICLE 1. The sole political party existing in Germany is the National Socialist German Workers' Party.

ARTICLE 2. Whoever shall undertake to maintain the organization of another party, or to found a new party, shall be punished with a sentence of hard labour of up to three years, or of prison between six months and three years, unless other regulations provide for heavier punishment.

Source D: Law Concerning the Head of the German State, 1 August 1934.

The government has passed the following law, which is being proclaimed herewith:

ARTICLE 1. The office of President shall be combined with that of Chancellor. Thus all the functions heretofore exercised by the President are transferred to the Führer and Chancellor Adolf Hitler. He has the right to appoint his deputy.

ARTICLE 2. This law is in force as of the date of the death of President von Hindenburg.

Source E: from a newspaper article by Ernst Rohm, June 1933.

A tremendous victory has been won. But not absolute victory! . . . In the new Germany the disciplined brown storm battalions of the German revolution stand side by side with the armed forces . . . The SA and SS are the foundation pillars of the coming National Socialist State – their State for which they have fought and which they will defend . . . The SA and SS will not tolerate the German revolution going to sleep or being betrayed at the half-way stage by non-combatants . . . the brown army [so called because of the SA uniforms] is the last levy of the nation, the last bastion against Communism.

Source F: from the Prosecutor's speech at the Nuremberg Trial 1946.

On 24th March 1933, only 535 out of the regular 747 deputies of the Reichstag were present. The absence of some was unexcused; they were in protective custody in concentration camps. Subject to the full weight of the Nazi pressure and terror, the Reichstag passed an enabling act known as the 'Law for the Protection of the People and the State', with a vote of 441 in favour.

. . . Thus the Nazis acquired full political control, completely unrestrained by any provision of the Weimar Constitution.

Questions

*1. (i) Explain the reference to the Reichsrat (Source B). [2]
    (ii) What title was given for the combination of Chancellor and President (Source D)? [1]
2. To what extent were the principles in Source B based on those in Source A? [4]
3. How accurately does Source E describe the role of the SA and SS in the changes made in Germany between 1933 and 1934? [5]
4. What questions might the historian wish to ask about Source F as evidence for the political changes in Germany in 1933? [5]
5. Using these sources, and your own knowledge, comment on the validity of the description of Hitler's constitutional changes between 1933 and 1934 as a 'legal revolution'. [8]

Worked answer

*1. [Questions based on factual knowledge and allocated only a few marks should be covered as quickly as possible. Where one mark is available, the answer can often be provided in a word or phrase.

Where two are allocated, two or more separate points need to be made.]

(i) The Reichsrat was the part of the German legislature which represented the *Länder* or states. It was a non-elected chamber, members being appointed by the state governments.

(ii) Führer.

SOURCES

2. THE FUNCTIONING OF POLITICAL INSTITUTIONS IN NAZI GERMANY

Source G: from a communication from the Minister of the Interior to the Chancellor, 4 June 1934.

If we are to stick to the idea of a central and unified leadership of the Reich through the Reich Chancellor and the departmental ministers assisting him, who corporately together with the Reich Chancellor form the Reich Government, then it is impossible to leave differences of opinion between a departmental minister on the one hand and a governor on the other . . . to be decided by the Reich Chancellor. On the contrary, the decision of the Reich Minister who represents the Reich Government in his area of responsibility must be accepted by the Reich Governor without allowing him a form of legal redress against the decision of the Reich Minister in the field of legislation.

Source H: from a communication between the Chancellor and the Minister of the Interior, 1934.

The Reich Chancellor agrees that, generally speaking, differences of opinion between a departmental minister and a Reich Governor on the legality or expediency of a State law cannot be left to his decision. In the Chancellor's view an exception must be made for those cases which are concerned with questions of special political importance. In the view of the Reich Chancellor such a regulation is consistent with his position of leadership.

Source I: from a statement by Werner Willikens, State Secretary in the Reich Ministry of Agriculture, to a meeting of state agricultural representatives, February 1934.

Everyone who has the opportunity to observe it knows that the Führer can hardly dictate from above everything which he intends to realize sooner or later. On the contrary, up till now everyone with a post in the new Germany has worked best when he has, so to speak, worked towards the Führer. Very often . . . it has been the case . . . that individuals have simply waited for orders and instructions. Unfortunately, the same will be true in the future; but in fact it is the duty of everybody to try to work towards the Führer along the lines he would wish. Anyone who makes mistakes will notice it soon enough. But anyone who really works towards the Führer along his lines and towards his goal will certainly both now and in the future one day have the finest reward in the form of the sudden legal confirmation of his work.

Source J: from an article 'Party and State', appearing in a legal journal on 19 May 1936. The author, Walter Sommer, was a civil servant in the Department for Affairs of State.

A. Party and State form, it is true, a unity, but they are not a single entity, not one and the same thing. Party and State have different tasks and to fulfil these different tasks have separate administrations, separate laws, and separate judicial systems.

B. The Führer defined the respective tasks of Party and State in bold and clear strokes in the final speech of the Party Congress in 1935. This declaration will be the basis of the future State law.

(*a*) The Party has the task of leading people and educating them in the way needed by the National Socialist State for the realization of its goals.

(*b*) The State has the task of administration. The State administration is specifically excluded from interference by the Party.

(*c*) A degree of influence by the Party on the State administration has, however, been secured for a transitional period. The Führer considers this transitional period as necessary so long as the State apparatus has not yet been transformed along Party lines . . .

(d) It is the Führer's wish that the Party should exert influence on the State only in ways which are legally sanctioned. Party offices must not interfere directly with the work of government bodies. All complaints about the State administration must be forwarded to the responsible Reich Minister via the mediator between Party and State appointed by the Fuhrer – his deputy, Reich Minister Hess.

(e) The strongest pressure on the State administration to gear itself to the Party lies in the Führer's statement: tasks which the State cannot fulfil will, if necessary, be transferred to the Party.

C. The Party is independent of the State even in its administration, its jurisdiction and in its legal system . . . The Party is not under any kind of State supervision, it also does not owe its existence to any kind of State decree.

Source K: from the Memoirs of Otto Dietrich, Hitler's press chief; published in 1955.

In the twelve years of his rule in Germany Hitler produced the biggest confusion in government that has ever existed in a civilized state. During his period of government, he removed from the organization of the state all clarity of leadership and produced a completely opaque network of competencies. It was not laziness or an excessive degree of tolerance which led the otherwise energetic and forceful Hitler to tolerate this real witch's cauldron of struggles for position and conflicts over competence. It was intentional. With this technique he systematically disorganized the upper echelons of the Reich leadership in order to develop and further the authority of his own will until he became a despotic tyrant.

Questions

1. (i) What were the alternative title and the main function of the Reich Governor (Source H)? [2]
    (ii) Explain the meaning of 'produced a completely opaque network of competencies' (Source K). [2]
*2. What can be inferred from Source I about the problems which the State Secretary in the Reich Ministry of Agriculture was attempting to resolve? [4]
3. In what ways are the views expressed in Sources G, H and J (i) similar and (ii) different to each other? [5]
4. How useful and reliable would Source K be to the historian studying the political structure of Nazi Germany? [5]
5. According to Haffner, Hitler's power over the Nazi political and administrative system was based on his use of 'controlled chaos'. Comment on this view in the light of Sources G to K and your own knowledge. [7]

Worked answer

*2. [The answer to this question needs to be confined entirely to the material in the Source. At the same time, the reasoning behind the statements should be analysed. The emphasis therefore needs to be on inferences from the Source rather than supplements to it.]

The advice provided to agricultural representatives by Secretary of State Willikens is expressed in a positive way; this would, however, have been a response to certain negative perceptions. The initial statement that 'the Führer can hardly dictate from above everything' would have been a criticism of those who expected constant and direct leadership. Hence those who 'simply waited for orders and instructions' would need to be more willing to exercise their initiative. At the same time, any such responsibility would need to be more in accordance with the official policy. Closer co-ordination was therefore necessary since 'it is the duty of everybody to try to work towards the Führer along the lines he would wish'. There is also an implied criticism of the low level of some of the work carried out since the Secretary of State saw it as necessary to point out that those making mistakes 'will notice it soon enough'. The overall tenor of the Source is the need for greater responsibility in decision-making, undertaken in the spirit of proper delegation: this would receive 'the finest reward' through 'sudden legal confirmation'.

3

INDOCTRINATION, PROPAGANDA AND TERROR

BACKGROUND NARRATIVE

The application of Nazi ideas and ideology depended on two types of force against individuals and social groups. One of these took the form of indoctrination and propaganda, the other was based on terror.

As we have seen in Chapter 2, the Nazis maintained the basic institutional structure of the Weimar Republic while adding a nazified layer. The same applied to the process of indoctrination and propaganda. The Ministry of Education was fully centralised as part of the campaign to destroy the autonomy of the *Länder* in 1933. It sought to nazify schools through the imposition of a common curriculum which introduced new subjects closely related to Nazi ideology. Meanwhile, a new institution had been established in March 1933 in the form of the Ministry of People's Enlightenment and Propaganda. Presided over by Goebbels, this aimed at the population at large. It controlled all areas of propaganda through radio, films and the press, and influenced cultural output in the form of literature, music and the fine arts. Another vehicle for propaganda was the 1936 Law on the Hitler Youth, which confirmed the existence of an institution which had existed since the establishment of the Third Reich.

The other side of the coin was the control of the German people through coercion and, if necessary, terror. This was the responsibility of the part of the system generally known as the SS/Gestapo/SD complex. The Schutzstaffeln (Security Squads SS), formed in 1925, merged with the SD and the Gestapo to assume complete responsibility for security and political policing. The SS complex also did more than any other institution within Germany to implement Hitler's racial policies and, from 1941, became the instrument of genocide. (See later.)

The individual Nazi leaders most responsible for these developments were Goebbels and Himmler. Both aimed to implement Hitler's racial ideas and indeed to give some structure to them. But their methods differed. Goebbels operated within the regular institutions of the Nazi State, while Himmler sought to transcend them by creating a new system.

ANALYSIS (1): HOW EFFECTIVE WERE INDOCTRINATION AND PROPAGANDA?

Goebbels said at a press conference establishing the Ministry of People's Enlightenment and Propaganda on 15 March 1933: 'It is not enough for people to be more or less reconciled to our regime, to be persuaded to adopt a neutral attitude towards us; rather we want to work on people until they have capitulated to us, until they grasp ideologically that what is happening in Germany today not only must be accepted but also can be accepted.'[1] He also emphasised the need to take full advantage of the latest technology in order to achieve maximum saturation to create complete loyalty and subservience.

Such a programme clearly required a considerable administrative infrastructure. The main requirement was the overall co-ordination of the transmission of ideology and influences. This was accomplished by two changes. The first was an increase in the power of an existing institution, the Ministry of Education. This was fully centralised to remove the initiative from the individual *Länder*; particularism, after all, was likely to be the main threat to achieving educational conformity. The second was the establishment of the Ministry for People's Enlightenment and Propaganda. In theory this was all-embracing. With additions made during the course of 1933, it eventually comprised a series of Chambers, including those for press, radio, theatre, music, creative arts and film. In theory the regime had the power to apply negative censorship in whatever form it considered necessary and, more constructively, to shape the development of culture at all levels.

In assessing the impact of these institutions, a distinction needs to be made between propaganda and indoctrination. To an extent these were connected, since the long-term indoctrination of the population involved regular exposure to official propaganda. Yet propaganda was on the whole more directly related to the use of channels such as the radio, cinema and press, while indoctrination was a process carried out in education, the youth movements, the work place and the armed forces. Propaganda provided the highlights, indoctrination the main body.

Indoctrination as a long-term process could be most effectively applied to Germany's youth. The methods used of indoctrinating youth were nothing if not thorough. Schools experienced a radicalisation of the curriculum which saw the introduction of race study, eugenics and health biology, all used as vehicles for imparting Nazi ideology. Conventional subjects, such as History and even Mathematics were given a twist: they were geared at every possible opportunity to enhancing Nazism. For example, twenty-two out of the seventy-six pages of the official Mathematics textbook contained ideological references such as calculations of the cost to produce lunatic asylums as opposed to workers' housing.[2] Another radical departure was the preparation of boys and girls for separate and obviously stereotyped roles. The teaching profession was also carefully organised, the Nazi Teachers' League (NSLB) accounting for 97 per cent of the total teaching force by 1937.

And yet the process was in many ways badly flawed. Education experienced the sort of overlapping between administrative and party organs which has already been examined in Chapter 2. For example, the Ministry of Education continued to use the guidelines of the Weimar Republic largely because it argued interminably with the Party headquarters about the shape to be taken by their replacement. The conflict between Ley and Rust on the one hand and Bormann and Hess on the other meant that the new regulations for elementary education were delayed until 1939, while secondary schools were served little better. This had two unfortunate side-effects. One was that the content of the curriculum was diluted by more traditional influences than was originally intended. The other was the persistence of confusion within the schools themselves as to the precise means of delivering the curriculum. Gestapo reports contained numerous examples of unsatisfactory teachers, many of whom were quite probably confused rather than deliberately uncooperative.

Indoctrination through a revised curriculum was complemented and reinforced by mobilisation through the youth movements. At least, this was the theory behind the specialised activities provided, according to age and gender, through the German Young People (DJ), Hitler Youth (HJ), Young Maidens (JM) and League of German Maidens (BDM). In some respects these carried widespread appeal, initially appearing as a challenge to more conservative forms of authority and giving youth a sense of collective power. But again the process suffered through administrative imbalance. This time there were arguments between the Ministry of Education and the Reich Youth Leadership as to underlying objectives and overriding priorities. Consequently the Hitler Youth and the educational system often diverged. The whole system also began to lose the edge of its initial appeal as it was seen to be enforcing the ideas of the new establishment. This trend was accelerated as the Hitler Youth became merely a nursery for military mobilisation. As the best of the youth leaders moved into the army, the official youth programme became more routine and less imaginative.

In general, education and the youth movement both lacked a completely clear exposition of ideology which, as in other spheres, remained eclectic. As Peukert maintains: 'the ideological content of National Socialism remained too vague to function as a self-sufficient educational objective. In practice young people selected from competing information-sources and values which were on offer.'[3] As it turned out, the impact of war meant that the more positive elements of the Hitler Youth disappeared altogether, while youth movements became increasingly influential. In this respect Nazi Germany – albeit unintentionally – gave birth to modern youth culture not as an integral part of conformity but as an autonomous and sometimes hostile response to it. Nothing could have been further from the intention of the Nazi leadership.

If indoctrination had a significant but limited impact on youth, could the same be said about the effect of propaganda on the rest of the population? A further distinction needs to be made at this point between the development of propaganda channels, such as radio, cinema and press, and the attempts to influence cultural output in literature, art and music.

The Nazis gave priority to the radio since this increased the impression of personal contact between the people and their leader, thereby enhancing the effectiveness of the Führer cult. Increased access to radio sets was, of course, an essential prerequisite for the success of this approach. This was achieved, with ownership of sets increasing from 25 per cent of households in 1932 to 70 per cent by 1939, the largest proportion anywhere in the world. For the vast majority of the population the radio provided the most abiding impression of the Führer that they were ever likely to have. As such this component of propaganda must go down as a considerable success.

Film proved a more difficult medium, and the regime used it less effectively than they did the radio. The most accomplished film was not necessarily the most influential. Riefenstahl's *Triumph of the Will* was commissioned by Hitler himself as a record of the Nuremberg rallies of 1934. Technically a brilliant achievement, it created a multi-layered image of Nazism which brought in all elements of society and directly fostered the Führer cult. On the other hand, it was too long for most audiences, who sometimes reacted negatively to the repetition of the same types of scene. During the war, film-based propaganda was radicalised and the anti-semitic component became more extreme. But it soon became apparent that Hitler's vision of what was likely to engage the public was less effective than Goebbels's. *The Eternal Jew*, commissioned by Hitler and directed by Hippler, was so crude that audiences were repelled by the images created. The anti-semitic message was conveyed more effectively through a feature film, *Jew Süss (Jud Süss)*. By this stage, Goebbels had learned how to intro-duce propaganda as a subliminal message within the context of a story with which the viewers could identify. This applied also to his attempts to engender a spirit of resistance to the Allies with his film on Frederick the Great. But such developments came too late for anything but a peripheral effect on the morale of a population facing imminent defeat.

Channelling the press for propaganda was also problematic. Because it was based on a more traditional technology, it had had longer than the radio to develop within the structure of private ownership; radio, by contrast, could be taken over relatively easily by the State. The proliferation of newspapers during the liberal era of the Weimar Republic accentuated the difficulty: by 1933 there were about 4,700 daily newspapers in Germany, representing a wide variety of political and regional views and loyalties. To an extent, the regime achieved effective administrative control. Between 1933 and 1945, for example, the number of State-owned newspapers increased from 2.5 per cent of the total to 82 per cent. The German News Agency (DNB) provided an effective control over the means whereby news was to be presented; news agencies were amalgamated to ensure a single source of information; and journalists were made responsible to the State rather than to their editors. But the result was a bland form of journalism which produced a decline in public interest. Throughout the period, the regime was never able to use the press to generate support.

The emphasis of its censorship was therefore preventive rather than creative.

The Nazi relationship with culture was ambivalent. On the one hand, it distrusted some of the traditional content while, on the other, never quite succeeding in providing an alternative. In the three major cases of literature, art and music, censorship created a contemporary vacuum which a new and distinctive Nazi culture was intended to fill. The results differed in intensity. Literature produced a complete void; music was less affected; and the vacuum of art was most filled – but with work of distressingly low quality.

The focus on literature was preventive censorship. This meant the massive book-burning sessions in which the SA took part, and the removal of over 2,500 German authors from the approved lists. To some extent destruction was cathartic. It could never seriously have been the preliminary to an alternative Nazi literature since Nazism itself was anti-intellectual. It discouraged any diversity of viewpoints and individual experience, seeking instead to stereotype collectivism. Within this atmosphere any chance of creating an 'official' literature disappeared – even supposing that the population would have been allowed any time to read it.

If the Nazis gave up on literature as a form of propaganda, they made a deliberate effort to use the visual arts to put across basic blood and soil values. Painters like Kampf and Ziegler were able to provide pictorial stereotypes of physical appearance, of women as mothers and home-minders, and of men in a variety of martial roles. Such images reinforced the roles inculcated through the institutions of youth indoctrination, such as the BDM and the HJ. On the other hand, the result was a form of art which was bland and lacking in any obvious talent. The vacuum produced by preventive censorship was filled with mediocrity. Much of the 'Nazi' art was derivative and eclectic: for example, Kamp's study of Venus and Adonis was a thinly disguised copy of earlier masters such as Rubens and David. The effect of such plagiarism on the public cannot have been anything more than peripheral, especially since there was always more interest in exhibitions of non-Nazi art which were officially classed as 'degenerate'.

The Nazi regime ended the period of musical experimentation which had been a major cultural feature of the Weimar Republic. The works of Schoenberg and Berg were considered un-German, while those of Mendelssohn were banned as 'Jewish'. Yet the majority of German or Austrian composers were unaffected and retained their place as part of Germany's cultural heritage. The Nazis did, however, use certain composers as the spearhead of their cultural penetration: foremost among these was Wagner, whose *Ring* cycle was seen by Hitler as the musical embodiment of *völkisch* values. Contemporary composers like Richard Strauss and Carl Orff had ambivalent attitudes. They managed to coexist with the regime and produce work which outlived the Reich. In this sense the quality of the Reich's musical output was superior to the work of painters like Kampf and Ziegler, but the result was less distinctively Nazi. Overall, Nazi culture was ephemeral and, unlike Socialist Realism in Russia, had no lasting impact on culture.

The ultimate test of the success of Nazi propaganda must be the degree to which the people of Germany could be brought to accept the experience of war. Throughout the Nazi era there were really two levels of propaganda. One level put across Hitler's basic ideology, the other made pragmatic adjustments to fit the needs of the moment. During the period 1933–9, pragmatism frequently diluted ideology, giving rise to considerable theoretical inconsistency in Hitler's ideas. During this period Hitler was presented as a man of peace and yet all the processes of indoctrination and propaganda emphasised struggle and its martial refinement. The period 1939–45 tended to bring together more completely the man and his ideas. This occurred in two stages. The first was the acclimatisation of the people to the idea of war, achieved through the emphasis on *Blitzkrieg*, or 'lightning' war. Logically this fitted in with the notion of easy conquest achieved by the 'master race', and while it lasted it was a considerable success: Hitler probably reached the peak of his popularity in 1940, at the time of the fall of France. During the second stage, however, propaganda had to acclimatise the people to the experience of war. At first Goebbels scored a propaganda success in his 'total war' speech in 1943 but, in the longer term there was a clear decline in popular enthusiasm. From 1943 the main characteristic shown by German civilians was fortitude in the face of adversity and destruction, not a fanatical desire to achieve a world vision. By this stage, Nazi propaganda and indoctrination had not so much failed. They had become irrelevant.

Questions

1. How did the Nazi regime see the connection between indoctrination and propaganda?
2. 'The Nazi regime failed as an instrument of indoctrination and propaganda.' Is this true?
3. Was there a Nazi cultural revolution?

ANALYSIS (2): HOW FAR WAS THE NAZI REGIME DOMINATED BY THE SS STRUCTURE?

The SS comprised a complex set of institutions collectively known as the SS/Gestapo/SD complex. It grew from comparatively small origins to provide, in the view of Noakes and Pridham 'a separate organizational framework for the enforcement of the will of the regime'.[5] The following analysis is based on the general premise that this framework did come to dominate the regime but that it suffered nevertheless from several inherent faults.

The SS complex grew from three separate strands to form a network which covered all areas of policing and security. The three were initially separate. The SS (Schutzstaffeln) originated in 1925 as the elite within the SA; Himmler took over its leadership in 1929. The SD (Sicherheitsdienst) was set up in 1931 as the NSDAP's internal police force. The Gestapo (short for Geheime Staatspolizei, or secret state police) was established in Prussia by Goering in April 1933 and was initially accountable to the Ministry of the Interior. Gradually these components came together as the SS infiltrated the leading positions of the State police system. In November 1934, Goering recognised Himmler as the effective head of the Gestapo. The process was confirmed when Himmler was appointed Reichsführer SS: Hitler's decree of 17 June 1936 was 'to unify the control of police duties in the Reich'. From this stage onwards the SS expanded even further. They penetrated the army by means of the SS Special Service Troops (SS-Verfügungstruppe – SS TV), from which were eventually recruited the military units, the Waffen SS. They took over from the SA the organisation of the concentration camps, staffing them with the Death's Head Formations (SS-Totenkopfverbände – SS-TV), while the genocide programme from 1941 came under the control of the Reich Security Main Office (Reichssicherheitshauptamt or RSHA).

This pattern of growth gradually altered the overall balance of the Nazi state. At first the regime was a compromise between party influences on the one hand and the traditional forces in the administration, army and business. In 1933 and 1934, the period of the so-called 'legal revolution', the SS played a subordinate role. From the end of 1934 onwards, however, the SS became the principal agent in the process of radicalisation. Although linked with State and party structures, the SS became independent of both. Then, during the period of war, the SS organised the whole network of conquered territories as well as the programmes for slave labour and extermination. This has led some historians to believe that by 1941 the Nazi State had been transformed into an SS State.

While extending the area of its administrative competence, the SS became the guardian of the race and struggle ideology of the Nazi movement and was consistently the main force behind its radicalisation. This showed itself in a number of ways. As early as 1931 the SS Marriage Order aimed 'to create a hereditarily healthy clan of a strictly Nordic German type'.[4] In some respects, Himmler went even further than Hitler. This applied especially to his views on Christianity. In 1937 he sanctioned the view that 'It is part of the mission of the SS to give the German people over the next fifty years the non-Christian ideological foundations for a way of life appropriate to their character'.[5] The SS also maintained the racial emphasis of the *Volksgemeinschaft* ('people's community') far more completely than did any of the institutions of the Nazi State, which tended to follow a more pragmatic course. It could be argued that Himmler and Goebbels, much as they disliked each other personally, were complementary in realising the racial mission of Nazism. Only Goebbels hoped to achieve it through the institutional structure of the State, while Himmler sought to transcend the State altogether.

Yet, for all its influence and effectiveness, there were certain deficiencies within the SS/Getapo/SD complex. The strongest criticism has been made by Höhne, who believes that 'the SS world was a bizarre nonsensical affair, devoid of all logic . . . history shows that the SS was anything but an organization constructed and directed on some diabolically efficient system: it was the product of accident and automatism. The real history of the SS is a story of idealists and criminals, of place-seekers and romantics: it is the history of the most fantastic association of men imaginable.'[6] This probably goes too far: after all, might the last point not apply to the story of Nazism generally? But given that the 'fantastic' occurred, the SS was a vital structural part in its realisation: this surely makes more sense than seeing it as a fantastic part of the Nazi system. The identification of deficiencies therefore needs to be more specific.

These might include the perpetual conflict between Himmler and other Nazi leaders such as Goering, Frank and Bormann. Or, within the SS, attention could be drawn to the growing differences between the racial 'idealism' of Himmler and the more ruthless and self-seeking opportunism of Heydrich. More fundamentally, the SS structure could be criticised for its enormous complexity, for its constant shifts, changes of shape and subdivisions. Historians have also questioned the extent to which these sub-structures within the SS complex were fully competent.

The most recent target has been the Gestapo. Along with the Soviet

KGB, the Gestapo became the twentieth century's epitome of the effective and all-embracing totalitarian police force affecting the entire population. How true is this picture? On the one hand, the Gestapo has been seen as a success story. Crankshaw, for example, considered them a 'highly professional corps'.[7] According to Schülz 'scarcely a politically significant initiative against the National Socialist regime went undetected'.[8] Delarue maintains: 'Never before, in no other land and at no other time, had an organisation attained such a comprehensive penetration of society, possessed such power.'[9] On the other hand, recent views have stressed that the reputation of the Gestapo is a myth which derives from its own propaganda. Heydrich, for example, said in 1941: 'The secret police, the criminal police and the security forces are shrouded in the whispered secrets of the political crime novel.'[10] In fact, argue Mallman and Paul, the Gestapo were insufficiently equipped to carry out the directives issued centrally and that they relied increasingly on information volunteered by members of the public. This has been based largely on local studies which show that 'the Gestapo at local level was hardly an imposing detective organization, but rather an under-staffed, under-bureaucratized agency, limping along behind the permanent inflation of its tasks'.[11] This applied especially to Stettin, Koslin, Hanover, Bremen, Dortmund, Düsseldorf, Würzburg and other areas. The beginning of the war aggravated the problem with a further decline in the number of staff. Inexperienced officials replaced those who had been conscripted, and the use of torture tended to increase, along with general thuggery. The factor which made the Gestapo function even as effectively as it did was the large number of denunciations which came from a large part of the population. The total membership of the Gestapo even by the end of 1944 was little more than 32,000, of which only half were fully concerned with the task of political policing.[12]

It is indeed quite possible that the effectiveness of the Gestapo was susperseded by the East German police force the Stasi, itself directly influenced by the Soviet KGB. This is a clear indication that the totalitarian policing methods of Stalin's Russia were more effective than those of Hitler's Germany. But the Soviet Union had no equivalent to the SS, the most completely totalitarian part of the Nazi regime. Certainly Himmler came closer than the official administration to giving effect to the incoherent ramblings of Hitler's *Mein Kampf*.

Questions

1. Why was the development of the SS structure so complicated?
2. Was the SS the logical development of the Nazi State system
   – or a 'bizarre' departure from it?
3. Was the Gestapo a failure?

SOURCES

1. THE ORGANIZATION OF PROPAGANDA

Source A: from a speech by Goebbels, 15 March 1933.

The most important tasks of this Ministry must be the following. Firstly, all propaganda ventures and all institutions for the enlightenment of the people throughout the Reich and the states must be centralized in one hand. Furthermore, it must be our task to instil into these propaganda facilities a modern feeling and bring them up to date. Technology must not be allowed to proceed ahead of the Reich; the Reich must go along with technology. Only the most modern things are good enough. We are living now in an age when the masses must support policies . . . It is the task of State propaganda so to simplify complicated ways of thinking that even the smallest man in the street may understand.

Source B: Goebbels speaking to a meeting of radio officials on 25 March 1933.

The Ministry has the task of achieving a mobilization of mind and spirit in Germany. It is, therefore, in the sphere of the mind what the Defence Ministry is in the sphere of defence. Thus, this ministry will require money and will receive money because of a fact which everybody in the Government now recognizes, namely that the mobilization of the mind is as necessary as, perhaps even more necessary than, the material mobilization of the nation.

Source C: from the local paper in Neu-Isenberg near Frankfurt, 16 March 1934.

Attention! The Führer is speaking on the radio. On Wednesday 21 March, the Führer is speaking on all German stations from 11.00 to 11.50 a.m. According to a regulation of the Gau headquarters, the district Party headquarters has ordered that all factory owners, department stores, offices, shops, pubs and blocks of flats put up loudspeakers an hour before the broadcast of the Führer's speech so that the whole work force and all national comrades can participate fully in the broadcast. The district headquarters expects this order to be obeyed without exception so that the Führer's wish to speak to his people can be implemented.

Source D: from official instructions issued at the daily press conferences in the Propaganda Ministry.

6.iv.35: The Propaganda Ministry asks us to put to editors-in-chief the following requests, which must be observed in future with particular care.

Photos showing members of the Reich Government at dining tables in front of rows of bottles must not be published in future, particularly since it is known that a large number of the Cabinet are abstemious. Ministers take part in social events for reasons of international etiquette and for strictly official purposes, which they regard merely as a duty and not as a pleasure. Recently, because of a great number of photos, the utterly absurd impression has been created among the public that members of the Government are living it up. News pictures must therefore change in this respect.

Source E: from a description by Louis P. Lochner, head of the Associated Press Bureau in Berlin, May 1933.

The whole civilized world was shocked when on the evening of 10 May 1933 the books of authors displeasing to the Nazis, including those of our own Helen Keller, were solemnly burned on the immense Franz Josef Platz between the University of Berlin and the State Opera on Unter den Linden. I was a witness to the scene.

All afternoon Nazi raiding parties had gone into public and private libraries, throwing on to the streets such books as Dr Goebbels in his supreme wisdom had decided were unfit for Nazi Germany. From the streets Nazi columns of beer-hall fighters had picked up these discarded volumes and taken them to the square above referred to.

Here the heap grew higher and higher, and every few minutes another howling mob arrived, adding more books to the impressive pyre. Then, as night fell, students from the university, mobilized by the little doctor, performed veritable Indian dances and incantations as the flames began to soar skyward.

Source F: from an article in the *Daily Express*, written by David Lloyd George, 17 November 1936.

I have just returned from a visit to Germany . . . I have now seen the famous German Leader and also something of the great change he has effected.

. . . It is true that public criticism of the Government is forbidden in every form. That does not mean that criticism is absent. I have heard the speeches of prominent Nazi orators freely condemned.

But not a word of criticism or of disapproval have I heard of Hitler. He is as immune from criticism as a king in a monarchical country.

Questions

1. (i) What was the full name of 'this Ministry' (Source A)? [1]
   (ii) What was the Gau, referred to in Source C? [1]
2. How far are the points expressed in Sources B and C a logical application of the ideas expressed in Source A? [5]
3. To what extent does Source D show the ease with which the Nazi regime was able to control the German press? [5]
*4. How do the language and tone used in Source E show the viewpoint of the author of the events he describes? [4]
5. Using Sources A to F and your own knowledge, would you agree that the creation of loyal Nazis was achieved by 'negative' rather than by 'positive' means? [8]

Worked answer

*4 [In this question, marks are allocated to three components, the author's 'viewpoint' as revealed by the 'language' and 'tone'. 'Language' refers to specific words and phrases, 'tone' to the overall impression created by these words and phrases. Both should be covered.]

The viewpoint of the author is one of deep hostility to the book-burning episode in Berlin. Those who took part are described contemptuously as 'raiding parties', 'beer-hall fighters', and 'howling mob'. The burning is given emphasis through words like 'pyre' and flames which 'soar skyward'. All this reinforces the tone, which is one of shock and outrage that such an important product of civilisation could be destroyed with such wanton abandon; the word 'pyre' has special significance here. The instigator, Dr Goebbels, comes in for some sarcastic treatment in the reference to 'his supreme wisdom'.

SOURCES

2. THE SECURITY SYSTEM OF THE SS

Source G: from the *Volkischer Beobachter (Munich Observer)*, 27 January 1936.

The Secret State Police is an official machine on the lines of the Criminal Police, whose special task is the prosecution of crimes and offences against the State, above all the prosecution of high treason and treason. The task of the Secret State Police is to detect these crimes and offences, to ascertain the perpetrators and to bring them to judicial punishment . . . The next most important field of operations for the Secret State Police is the preventive combating of all dangers threatening the State and the leadership of the State. As, since the National Socialist Revolution, all open struggle and all open opposition to the State and to the leadership of the State is forbidden, a Secret State Police as a preventive instrument in the struggle against all dangers threatening the State is indissolubly bound up with the National Socialist Leader State.

Source H: Heydrich on his promotion to Himmler's deputy, 1933:

Now we no longer need the Party. It has played its role and has opened the way to power. Now the SS must penetrate the police and create a new organisation there.

Source I: Himmler and the values of the SS in a speech at the Reich Peasant Congress on 12 November 1935.

The first principle for us was and is the recognition of the values of blood and selection . . . We went about it like a seedsman who, wanting to improve the strain of a good old variety which has become crossbred and lost its vigour, goes through the fields to pick the seeds of the best plants. We sorted out the people who we thought unsuitable for the formation of the SS simply on the basis of outward appearance.

The nature of the selection process was to concentrate on the choice of those who came physically closest to the ideal of nordic man. External features such as size and a racially appropriate appearance played and still play a role here . . .

The second principle and virtue which we tried to instil in the SS and to give to it as an indelible characteristic for the future is the will to freedom and a fighting spirit . . .

The third principle and virtue are the concepts of loyalty and honour . . .

The fourth principle and virtue that is valid for us is obedience, which does not hesitate for a moment but unconditionally follows every order which comes from the Führer or is legitimately given by a superior, obedience ... which obeys just as unconditionally and goes into the attack even when one might think on one's heart one could not bring oneself to do so.

Source J: Heydrich's attitude to the SS, as described by his wife during the 1950s.

Himmler was obsessed by ideas, kept developing new ones, at first only in theory, but then he tried to realize them. My husband did not play with ideas. His tasks were concrete and clear and depended on the day-to-day events. Naturally, he identified himself with the ideological framework. This framework was, however, regarded as self-evident and hardly bothered my husband, at least in those days. When he joined the SS the order had not yet become what Himmler with his ideas was to turn it into. Each person interpreted National Socialism as it suited them. There were as many ideologies as there were members. As far as my husband was concerned, the idea of a greater Germany naturally played a decisive role – the rebirth of Germany. But that was really something obvious rather than being a matter of ideology. The German nation was for him more a geographical rather than a racial concept and his concrete tasks developed with the tasks of the Reich as Hitler projected it.

Source K: Hitler's response to the plea of Frick (Minister of the Interior) for a regulation on who was to control the police, 17 June 1936.

To unify the control of police duties in the Reich, a chief of the German police shall be appointed within the Reich Ministry of the Interior, to whom is assigned the direction and executive authority for all police matters within the jurisdiction of the Reich and Prussian Ministries of the Interior.

1. The Deputy Chief of the Prussian Gestapo, Reichsführer SS Himmler, is hereby nominated Chief of the German police in the Reich Ministry of the Interior.
2. He is personally and directly subordinate to the Reich and Prussian Ministers of the Interior.
3. For matters within his jurisdiction he represents the Reich and Prussian Ministers of the Interior in the absence of the latter.
4. He carries the service title: Reichsführer SS and Chief of the German Police within the Reich Ministry of the Interior.

Source L: from a speech by Himmler to SS leaders in Posen, 4 October 1943.

One basic principle must be the absolute rule for the SS man: we must be honest, decent, loyal and comradely to members of our own blood and to nobody else. What happens to a Russian or a Czech does not interest me in the slightest. What the nations can offer in the way of good blood of our type we will take, if necessary by kidnapping their children and raising them here with us. Whether nations live in prosperity or kick the bucket interests me only in so far as we need them as slaves for our culture . . . Whether 10,000 Russian females fall down from exhaustion while digging an anti-tank ditch interests me only in so far as the anti-tank ditch is finished.

Questions

1 (i) What was the official German name, or abbreviation, for the 'Secret State Police' (Source G)? [1]

   (ii) What was the *Munich Observer* (Source G)? [1]

2 How much evidence is there in Sources H, I and J to support the view that ideology was more important to Himmler than to Heydrich? [5]

3 How useful and reliable would the historian find Source J as an insight into the role of Heydrich in the SS? [4]

4 How do Sources G and L differ in language and tone? How would you explain these differences? [6]

*5 Using Sources G to L, and your own knowledge, how true would it be to say that the SS became a 'state within a state'? [8]

Worked answer

*5. [It is important in the answer to this question to focus on the issue of 'state within a state' from the two directions of 'Sources G to L' and 'your own knowledge'. The most effective way of doing this and ensuring maximum marks is to use two separate paragraphs and to specify which material comes from the sources, and which from elsewhere.]

The sources show that the SS certainly seemed to expand into a role much greater than that originally given to it by the State. In theory, the SS were encompassed within the state institutions. Indeed, Source G emphasises the importance of the SS complex as 'a preventive instrument in the struggle against all dangers threatening the State.' However, Minister of the Interior Frick was clearly concerned about the emergence of a new power as a possible rival to the institutions of the State. This necessitated Hitler's rationalization of the 'control of police duties in the Reich' within 'the jurisdiction of the Reich and Prussian Ministers of the Interior' (Source K). This did not prevent the emergence of an organisation conscious of a separate identity – and of being an elite with a special mission to create racial purity, as shown by Himmler in Source I. Less ideological, but more blatant, was Heydrich's view that the SS might penetrate deeply into the State now that 'we no longer need the Party' (Source H).

Other material can be used to back the views of the sources. The way in which the SS evolved was itself an example of the growth of a huge power bloc within the State. Emerging from within the SA, it took over the SD and Gestapo (initially intended as the Prussian State police), before expanding its role in the Wehrmacht in the form of the Waffen SS. During the Second World War it was responsible for the implementation of the racial programme in its most extreme phase – the extermination of the Jews. It also administered the Eastern territories and therefore assumed direct responsibility for the implementation of *Lebensraum*. Historians have increasingly emphasised the conflict between State and Nazi institutions. The best example of this so-called polycratic tension is the growth of the SS from humble origins into almost total ascendancy.

4

SUPPORT AND OPPOSITION

ANALYSIS (1): HOW EXTENSIVE WAS THE SUPPORT FOR HITLER AND NAZISM?

Support can be either active or tacit, positive or negative. It can mean direct commitment through personal conviction or, alternatively, the absence of opposition through fear of the consequences. Both types existed in Nazi Germany.

The main reason for positive support was the personal popularity of Hitler. To many he was a direct successor to the populist vision of the Kaiser during the Second Reich. There had been no equivalent during the Weimar Republic, with the possible exception of Hindenburg. Hitler therefore filled a gap and greatly extended the leadership cult. His appeal also had a chameleon nature: he offered something different to each class and yet pulled them all together with the uniqueness of his own vision for the future. He struck a chord with the wide-spread disillusionment with the institutions, parties and leaders of the Weimar Republic. He had, of course, the considerable advantage of a monopoly of the media which was used for the processes of indoctrination and propaganda examined in Chapter 3. But in a sense Hitler transcended the image created by Goebbels. The main reason for his popularity – and this may seem surprising – was that he was seen as a moderate. After all, he made sure that his political changes were technically constitutional; he emphasised that he was upholding traditional virtues; and, at least until the late 1930s, he professed to be deeply religious. There was considerable unease about the Nazi movement, especially about the thuggish tendencies of some of its members like Röhm and Streicher. But Hitler was perceived as the moderate who would tame the radicals. For this reason, he was seen 'practically as a hero' after the Night of the Long Knives in 1934.[1] In addition to controlling extremism, Hitler also appeared to guarantee peace, using it as a constant theme in his speeches until 1939.

Part of Hitler's popularity came through his capacity to reassure. The rest was due to his ability to deliver results. To an extent he was fortunate. He benefited from a series of opportunities, which he seized. One was the cyclical upturn in the economy after 1933: this was projected to a grateful population as his doing. He gained considerable ground in his quest for revisionism: the population compared with the rather slow developments of the Stresemann era Hitler's success in remilitarising the Rhineland in 1936 and annexing Austria and the Sudetenland in 1938 – all without recourse to war. Even those with a vested interest in undermining Hitler's position admitted to the strength of his appeal. For example, the SPD in exile, SOPADE, drew up a number of reports, one of which stated that 'Many people are convinced that Germany's foreign-policy demands are justified and cannot be passed over. The last few days have been marked by big fresh advances in the Führer's personal reputation'.[2]

Not all Germans were taken in by the Führer cult; many saw through the projection of his image as an apparent moderate. Yet for those who were not swept along in professed support for the system, there were too many negative constraints on action. The constitutional changes had removed the possibility not only of voting for established opposition parties but even the possibility of setting up new ones. Besides, the step-by-step approach of the 'legal revolution' had made opposition appear increasingly illogical. Why should it be justifiable at one point when earlier steps taken by the Nazis within the same process had not been resisted? Hence opposition, once considered a vital component of democracy, now became synonymous with disloyalty and treason. As such, it came within the scope of the terror applied by the SS and Gestapo. This was intended both to create object lessons and to isolate individuals by smashing the organisation which might have given them voice. Terror worked well because it affected only a minority but, at the same time, promoted an unwillingness among the majority to speak out over issues which they considered did not immediately affect them. It made sense for most Germans to accept a trend which seemed inexorable rather than to make themselves a target for certain and terrible retribution.

Looking at the different sectors of the population has, in the past, produced a number of stereotypes. The upper and middle classes, for example, were seen as enthusiastic supporters of the regime, having brought Hitler to power in the first place. The working class, by contrast, were oppressed by the Nazi system and had to grow to accept it in the absence of the parties which they traditionally supported, the SPD and the KPD. The female population was repressed but compliant; youth became increasingly radical, even fanatical, and the army was split between fervent Nazi supporters and a substantial layer of higher officers, usually Prussian, who held the Nazis in barely concealed contempt. All this has now been modified by recent historical research.

The upper middle class, especially the business sector, had initially supported the Nazi Party out of fear of communism. During the Third Reich the great industrialists threw in their lot with Hitler because the regime delivered to them a disciplined workforce which was deprived of any effective means of collective bargaining. Although Marxist historians have tended to exaggerate the 'monopoly capital' influence on Nazism, there remains little doubt that the industrial barons and the regime saw eye to eye with each other. Mobilisation for war brought an even closer identity, and many major industrial enterprises, such as Krupp and I.G. Farben, became fully implicated in the worst excesses of Nazi occupation.

The bulk of the middle classes are more difficult to disentangle. Some benefited greatly from Nazi rule and became a key element in the support of the regime. But others were more marginalised. The latter included the small landowners or peasantry. Theirs was an ambiguous position. On the one hand, Hitler built up the peasantry as the basis of the Nazi blood-and-soil policy, therefore as the most crucial component of the *Volksgemeinschaft*. On the other hand, the peasantry probably experienced the least benefit from the economic recovery from 1933 and had to suffer interference from the State in the form of the Reich Entailed Law preventing the subdivision of estates. Nevertheless, any resentment remained quiescent and there was no direct opposition from this sector. Small businesses also had a mixed record. Those which were reasonably efficient thrived in the atmosphere of the mid-1930s, while those which were struggling went to the wall. Hence the successful artisanate tended to worship Hitler, while that sector which failed was in effect proletarianised and had to settle for being nazified through the Nazi institutions aimed at the working class. At least they were not absorbed into the Communist ethos, which remained a concern to them. The salary-earning and white-collar sector of society, the so-called 'new' middle class, were less attracted by the 'blood-and-soil' or 'small self-made man' ethos of the Nazi appeal. They were, however, more responsive to the increased opportunities which accompanied economic revival and the rapidly growing bureaucratic complex which was Nazi Germany. The Nazi State was administered by huge numbers of officials who sank their individual identity into an authoritarian and impersonal system.

It was once argued that the working class remained more resistant to Nazi influences under the *Volksgemeinschaft*. It is true that the workers were less affected than the middle classes by the Führer cult and that they benefited far less from the economic recovery after 1933. After all, their wages were pegged, their working hours increased and their contributions to the GNP unacknowledged. They therefore had cause for grievance. Yet the vast majority settled down into tacit support, becoming drawn into the activities and diversions offered by the 'Strength through Joy' (KdF) and 'Beauty of Labour' (SDA) movements. Much of the workforce acknowledged the regime as the source of their economic recovery. Mason argues that 'the Nazi economic "miracle"' convinced many workers that 'things were getting better, especially as, for most of them, the point of reference was not the best years of the Weimar Republic but the more recent depths of the Depression'.[3] In any case, the full-scale use of modern methods, including the assembly-line process, made individual action more and more difficult. The whole process was attenuated by the mobilisation for war, which meant that 'Firm integration into traditional socio-cultural milieux was shaken'.[4] This made possible a growing loyalty to the leadership among the very people who had once been suspicious of it. According to contemporary evidence from SOPADE reports, 'There is no mistaking the enormous personal gains in credibility and prestige that Hitler has made, mainly perhaps among workers'.[5]

Women were for many years seen by historians as a distinct group, forced into compliance to the Nazi regime. Recent historiography, to which major contributions have been made by women, has moved away from this approach by integrating them more fully into the mainstream of German life. As such, women would have experienced the full range of views about Hitler. Nazism would, on the one hand, have exercised an appeal based on the family and home, reinforced by improved provision for maternity and for family benefits. Against this, of course, was the resentment caused by the removal of women from many sectors of employment, especially the professions. But this was often offset by the creation of new roles within party and public organisations, with which many women became actively involved. Hence for some women the Nazi regime actually brought further opportunities than had been available under the Weimar Republic. This applied especially to women who had few formal qualifications but who wished to be involved in political activism. By 1935 about 11 million out of the country's 35 million females belonged to the Nazi Women's Movement (NS-Frauenschaft) and were willing to support the ideas and beliefs of Nazism. Not all of these were meekly subservient: some, who were actually Nazi activists, challenged the official line on gender subordination. For example, a Nazi feminist, Sophie Rogge-Berne, argued in 1937 that it was misguided to remove women from the professions since 'Women doctors could give aid and comfort to fatigued mothers. Women teachers would be most suited to instruct adolescent girls. Women jurists would be most qualified for dealing with cases involving children.'[6] Overall, women are now accredited with a more active role in Nazi Germany, although this places more emphasis on their complicity with, rather than their compliancy to, the regime.

The army has always been seen as largely dominated by the Nazi political system, but there has been some shift in interpretations concerning its complicity in German war crimes. The bulk of the army was systematically taken over. Until 1934 at least it always had the option of removing Hitler, and Hindenburg, of course, remained its commander-in-chief until his death. But Hitler won its support by stealth rather than by the confrontation preferred by Röhm who wished to submerge the field grey into the 'brown flood' of the SA. The army was grateful for the action taken by Hitler during the Night of the Long Knives and, on the death of Hindenburg, backed his claim to the presidency. The support of the army was also institutionalised to an unprecedented degree in an oath of allegiance, making any future opposition an act akin to treason: 'I swear before God to give my unconditional obedience to Adolf Hitler, Führer of the Reich and of the German People, Supreme Commander.'[7] But the influence went further. Every attempt was made to nazify the army through the adoption of the swastika insignia on uniforms and through a prolonged process of indoctrination. The introduction of the Waffen SS as the elite corps was considered crucial for the invasion and conquest of much of Europe. For many years the view was that it was the SS, not the Wehrmacht, which committed the atrocities in the occupied territories. More recent research, however, has shown that the army played an integral part in the shooting of civilians in Poland and the Ukraine. Indeed, Bartov has argued that even members of the working class, who had once supported the SPD or KPD, could be transformed into 'brutalized and fanaticized soldiers'.[8]

Overall, there has been a recent shift in interpretation about the extent to which the regime was voluntarily supported by the population. More emphasis is now placed on complicity at all levels. Three historians present a particularly disturbing picture. Mallman and Paul argue that the Gestapo relied predominantly on information volunteered by large numbers of people – from all sections of society, including the working class. Many Germans, it seems, were willing to denounce each other.[9] Goldhagen goes further by insisting that a substantial portion of the German army were willing agents in the slaughter of Jews in the Ukraine and Russia.[10] It is, of course, possible that the pendulum has swung too far in the other direction and that more notice needs to be taken of the opposition which developed to the regime. To this we now turn.

Questions

1. How 'genuine' was the support within Germany for Hitler and the Nazi regime?
2. Did the appeal of Hitler and the Nazi regime break class barriers?

ANALYSIS (2): WHAT WAS THE EXTENT OF THE OPPOSITION TO HITLER'S REGIME?

Much more attention has recently been focused by historians on opposition to the Hitler regime than was the case during the first three decades after 1945. This is due partly to the increase of specialist studies on all areas of the Third Reich and partly to the influential thesis that the Nazi system was less efficient than was originally thought. The incomplete nature of German totalitarianism meant that opposition was not only possible: it was a reality, and the Gestapo were fully aware of it. It took various forms, ranging, in order of seriousness, from every-day grumbling to complaints about specific issues, more general political activism and, most threatening of all, resistance. The authorities also became increasingly concerned about the growth of social deviance which threatened to undermine the re-education of Germany's youth.

Grumbling and minor dissent were quite widespread. Kershaw has argued that 'The acute perception of social injustice, the class-conscious awareness of inequalities . . . changed less in the Third Reich than is often supposed . . . The extent of disillusionment and discontent in almost all sections of the population, rooted in the socio-economic experience of daily life, is remarkable.'[11] There was considerable oral dissent about the lack of wage increases, or increased working hours, or compulsory activities within the KdF, or the increasing subordination of the consumer market to rearmament. Yet the type of discontent remained at a remarkably low key, certainly when compared with the resistance of the peasantry to collectivisation in the Soviet Union. There was little chance of discontent ever being converted into something stronger. SOPADE reports indicated that most grumbling was sparked by economic conditions, and not by more fundamental reservations about the nature of the regime. 'This is especially so among the *Mittelstand* and the peasantry. These social strata are least of all ready to fight seriously against the regime because they know least of all what they should fight for.'[12] Most Germans were therefore never likely to turn against a system which, for all its inconveniences, they still preferred to the Weimar Republic.

In contrast to undirected grumbling, several formal complaints were made about specific issues. These might involve individuals, small groups or major institutions. The Churches, for example, came into conflict with the regime on three occasions. One was Pastor Niemöller's objection to the establishment of the Confessing Church: from July 1933 the twenty-eight provincial Protestant churches or Landeskirchen were centralised into a single Reich Church, which was brought into the central administration and placed under Hans Kerrl as Minister of Church Affairs in 1935. The second instance was the Catholic protest against the government order to replace crucifixes by portraits of Hitler in Catholic schools. A third, and the most significant, stance was taken in opposition to the regime's euthanasia programme from 1939 onwards. These complaints varied in the degree of their success. The Protestant opposition was less likely to succeed than the Catholic, owing to the fragmentation of Protestantism into a number of different sects and the fundamental issue on which that opposition was being expressed: the regime could hardly be expected to reverse a major constitutional change. The Catholic Church, by contrast, was a centralised structure, with considerable capacity for exerting pressure at certain specific points. It succeeded over the two issues it contested: the programmes to nazify Catholic schools and to conduct the clandestine euthanasia programmes were both temporarily suspended. On the other hand, the more general complaints made by the Pope in his 1937 encyclical *Mit brennender Sorge* (*With Deep Anxiety*) that the regime had broken the provisions of the Concordat across the board were less likely to succeed. There is little doubt that Christianity proved most effective not as a general impetus for opposition but as a residue for the nation's conscience. Despite efforts at the end of the 1930s to eradicate it through the paganism of the Nazi Faith Movement, the majority of Germans remained either Catholic or

Protestant, and the incidence of church attendance actually increased after 1939.

The expression of more general opposition through political activism was confined largely to the Communists and Social Democrats, as might be expected from the two parties which had previously had the support of the larger part of the working class. The Communists continued to try to oppose the regime actively, but failed badly. This was due in part to the success of the Gestapo in identifying and eradicating Communist cells. As a result, something like 10 per cent of the whole Communist membership were killed, and Thälmann, the leader of the KPD, was arrested as early as 1933. The continuing conflict between Communists and Social Democrats meant fewer converts on the shop floor and made it easier for the Gestapo to acquire information. The Communists were also impeded by external constraints such as the foreign policy of Stalin which culminated in the highly pragmatic Nazi–Soviet Non-Aggression Pact of August 1939. It was not until 1941, when Hitler invaded the Soviet Union, that the Communists began to make a comeback, largely under the tutelage of Stalin, who switched his entire emphasis to the direct support of the KPD. The SPD, meanwhile, had been less directly involved in political activism. From its position in exile, SOPADE was organised by Ernst Schumacher, initially from Prague, then from Paris. They were generally more restrained and cautious than the KPD in their actions. They had the advantage of more accurate information on the state of support shown for the regime in the SOPADE reports. By and large neither they nor the Communists succeeded in making any major inroads into the working classes. As we have already seen, there was plenty of grumbling but little chance of persuading workers to risk their livelihood, families and lives in the expression of political opposition.

There were, however, small groups who were prepared to make such a sacrifice. The strongest form of opposition took the form of resistance, an attempt to remove the regime altogether. Realistically this could be done only by a coup since all the constitutional channels had been blocked by Hitler's so-called 'legal revolution' between 1933 and 1934. The key to any chance of success was the army. This had, however, been won over by the process of gradual nazification during the 1930s. Hence the only possibility was the defection of disillusioned elements and their linking up with individuals and groups prepared to risk everything on a political substitution. The army elements were always there. Ironically, they were nearly always members of the Prussian aristocracy, deeply conservative in their outlook and, in some instances, former enemies of the Weimar Republic. But this should not be taken to the usual extreme view that the conservative forces within the army were generally anti-Nazi. Many, as we have already seen, welcomed Nazism without reservation. This was one of the basic reasons for the failure of armed resistance: there was simply no depth in numbers to offset the failure of individual attempts like the Stauffenberg bomb plot. A few courageous individuals did become involved. General Beck tried to persuade the General Staff to remove Hitler in 1938, and also urged the British government to resist Hitler's demands over the Sudetenland. Rommel participated in the plot against Hitler's life, for which he was forced to commit suicide. Other leading members of the resistance movements were strongly conservative, comprising members of the traditional right, many of whom had served Hitler at one time or another. These included von Hassell, former German ambassador to Italy, as well as Goerdeler, von Koltke and von Wartenburg. Also closely involved were Christian groups such as the Kreisau Circle, which produced a programme entitled 'Principles for the New Order of Germany', and prominent churchmen like Dietrich Bonhoeffer. Ultimately, however, all such resistance failed in its objective – which was to replace Hitler's regime with a more democratic one and to negotiate an armistice with the Allies. There would be no repetition of the situation in October and November 1918, since Hitler himself was head of state and was not open to any attempts to do a deal. In any case, the Allies insisted on unconditional surrender, thereby removing an important component from the programme of the German resistance movement. Hence Nazism could be removed only by conquering armies, not by internal revolution.

One category of opposition greatly puzzled the authorities. Social deviance was most apparent among younger Germans, especially from the working class, and pointed to the deficiencies of the Hitler Youth as a channel of indoctrination. As the whole structure became more bureaucratised and less imaginative, some of the earlier attractions began to wear off. The Hitler Youth came to be seen increasingly as part of the establishment rather than as a rival to it. Hence there developed alternative, even oppositional, cultures and groups among youth. Deviant behaviour among adolescents during the Third Reich was much wider than was once thought. In 1942 the Reich Youth Leadership stated: 'The formation of cliques, i.e. groupings of young people outside the Hitler Youth, has been on the increase before and, particularly, during the war to such a degree that one must speak of a serious risk of the political, moral and criminal subversion of youth.'[13]

Examples included the Navajos, centred largely on Cologne, the Kittelbach Pirates of Oberhausen and Düsseldorf, and the Roving Dudes of Essen. These were all sub-groups within the broader Edelweiss Pirates. They were antagonistic to authority and in particular to the Hitler Youth, patrols from which they would ambush and beat up: indeed one of their slogans was 'Eternal War on the Hitler Youth'. They also defied restrictions on movement during the war by undertaking extensive hikes, and they maintained a much more liberal attitude to sexuality than the authorities liked. Some also supported the Allies during the war or offered help to German army deserters. Less militant and more cultural in its emphasis was the Swing Movement. This was aimed more against the cultural indoctrination of the Reich and it adopted influences from British and especially American jazz. This was particularly provocative to the authorities, who regarded jazz as 'negro music' and therefore as 'degenerate'. In all cases the authorities were seriously concerned – but frequently did not know what to do – apart from the occasional salutary public hanging of Edelweiss Pirates. At the same time, the activities of the Edelweiss Pirates and Swing Movements lacked the organisational edge to be anything more than an embarrassment to the regime. Social deviance was, therefore, never likely to amount to serious political opposition.

The overall deduction which can be drawn from these different strands is a complex one. In theory, the Nazi State was totalitarian in that it eradicated institutions allowing for the formal expression of dissent and opposition and then proceeded to use the SS and Gestapo to pick off individual manifestations of anti-Nazi behaviour. By and large this combined process was successful: there was, after all, never any real threat to the regime except for the occasional act of violence. And yet the fact that opposition did develop in such a variety of forms indicates that totalitarianism was only partly successful: perhaps this can be quantified as considerably more so than in Mussolini's Italy but somewhat less so than in Stalin's Russia. The regime frequently had to make concessions on specific issues; it faced a general increase in deviant behaviour; and, during the war, it provoked the coalescence of normally incompatible groups. It is possible to go further. Peukert argues that the *Volksgemeinschaft* had not been achieved by 1939 and that the internal harmony of the system needed increasingly to be maintained by diverting public opinion against minority groups whether inside or outside Germany. 'Terror accordingly bit ever deeper . . . from the margins of society into its heart.'[14]

Questions

1. How much genuine opposition was there within Germany to the Nazi regime?
2. 'The existence of internal opposition shows that Nazi Germany was not a fully totalitarian regime.' Discuss.

SOURCES

1. POPULAR SUPPORT?

Source A: an extract from *Mein Kampf*.

Mass assemblies are also necessary for the reason that, in attending them, the individual who felt himself formerly only on the point of joining the new movement, now begins to feel isolated and in fear of being left alone as he acquires for the first time the picture of a great community which has a strengthening and encouraging effect on most people. Brigaded in a company or battalion, surrounded by his companions, he will march with a lighter heart to the attack than if he had to march alone. In the crowd he feels himself in some way thus sheltered.

Source B: The dedication, by Goering, on the first page of a photograph album entitled *Adolf Hitler*, published in 1936.

My Führer, we are not able to express our thanks in words. Nor are we able to show our loyalty and affection for you in words. Our entire gratitude, love for, and trust in you, my Führer, is shining upon you today from hundreds of thousands of eyes. Today the entire nation, the entire people feels strong and happy, because in you not only the Führer but also the saviour of the nation has appeared.

Source C: from a report by SOPADE, 1934.

A general phenomenon that has been noticeable for some time is still evident: Hitler is generally exempted from criticism . . .

A correspondent from Berlin puts the point in more detail: 'In general we can say that Adolf Hitler is exempted from criticism, his aims are conceded as honourable and people think that he cannot be blamed for the mismanagement of his subordinates. This is partly the result of the systematic Führer propaganda, but is also undoubtedly the effect of his personality. His personality impresses simple people, and Hitler still has a lot of personal support among the workers.

Source D: from a report by SOPADE, 1935.

KdF events have become very popular. Even ordinary workers can afford these walking trips, since they are generally cheaper than private hikes.

Almost all national comrades rate KdF as one of National Socialism's really creditable achievements. KdF sport courses are enjoying greater and greater popularity, even among older people. Everyone can take part.

Source E: from a report by SOPADE, 1935.

It became clear that the effects of the economic crisis on the inward resistance of the workers were more appalling than had previously been thought. We see it time and time again: the most courageous illegal fighter, the most relentless antagonist of the regime, is usually the unemployed man who has no more to lose. Whereas if a worker gets a job after years out of work, then – however bad his pay and conditions – he at once becomes apprehensive. Now he does have something to lose, however little, and the fear of the renewed misery of unemployment is worse than the misery itself. The National Socialists have not conquered the factories. The standing of the National Socialist 'shop stewards' has constantly fallen, while that of the old free union works committees has risen in corresponding degree. But the National Socialists have destroyed the workers' self-confidence: they have crushed the forces of solidarity and crippled their will to resist.

Questions

*1. Explain the meaning of the following terms:
   (i) KdF (Source D). [2]
   (ii) SOPADE (Sources C, D and E). [2]
2. What comments might a western liberal make on the ideas in Source A? [4]
3. Compare the language and tone of Sources B and C. [4]
4. How useful and reliable would Sources C, D and E be to the historian studying the popularity of the Nazi regime? [5]
5. 'Support for Hitler after 1933 existed for a variety of different reasons.' Comment on this view in the light of these sources and of your own knowledge. [8]

Worked answer

*1. [The mark allocation is slightly different to those for Question 1 in other sections. Two marks indicate the need for two identifiable pieces of information – a basic definition and a brief explanation. One mark would suggest the definition alone.]

(i) 'Kraft durch Freude' (or 'Strength through Joy'). This was an organisation responsible for the welfare and involvement of the German workforce.

(ii) SOPADE stands for the Social Democratic Party in Exile. Its purpose was to gather information and promote resistance to the Nazi regime.

SOURCES

2. CATHOLIC OPPOSITION?

Source F: a public statement made by Bishop Berning, 21 September 1933.

The German bishops have long ago said Yes to the new State, and have not only promised to recognise its authority . . . but are serving the State with burning love and all our strength.

Source G: from an official report, 1937.

The fact is that thirty to forty villagers got into the unlocked school on the night of 6 January 1937 to hang the crucifix back in its old place. Against the explicit advice of the witness R. that the crucifix had been taken down by the order of the government and that the break-in would constitute a breach of the peace if they contravened this order, the accused B.A. (with the help of a ladder which he fetched), hung the crucifix right up beside the picture of the Führer, which had been put in this newly assigned place. Everyone then left the school.

The court of Rhaunen, on 9 January 1937, ordered a custodial sentence against B.A.

Source H: from the Papal Encyclical *With Burning Anxiety*, 14 March 1937.

With burning anxiety and mounting unease We have observed for some time the way of suffering of the Church, the growing harassment of the confessors who stay true to it in spirit . . .

He who singles out race, the people of the State, the form of State, the bearers of State power or other basic element of human social organisation . . . he who singles out such elements from this worldly scale of values and sets them up as the highest norm over all, including over religious values, and reverences them with idolatry, he distorts and falsifies the God-created, God-demanded order of things. Such a person is far from real belief in God and from a conception of life that corresponds to such a belief.

Source I: Cardinal Galen's protest against police measures, 13 July 1941.

'Justice is the state's foundation.' We lament, we regard with great concern, the evidence of how this foundation is being shaken today, how justice – that natural Christian virtue, which is indispensable to the orderly existence of every human society – is not being plainly implemented and maintained for all. It is not only for the sake of the rights of the Church, not only for that of the rights of the human personality, it is also out of love for our nation and out of our profound concern for our country that we beg, ask, demand: Justice! Who is there among us who does not fear for the survival of his home when the foundations are being sapped?

The regular courts have no say over the jurisdiction by decree of the Secret Police. Since none of us know of a way that might give us an impartial control over the measures of the Gestapo – its expulsions, its arrests, its imprisonment of fellow Germans in concentration camps – large groups of Germans have a feeling of being without rights, and what is worse, harbour feelings of cowardly fear. Great harm is being done to the German community in this way.

The obligation of my episcopal office to defend the moral order, and the loyalty to my oath, which I swore before God and the government's representative, to prevent to the best of my ability any harm that might come to the German body politic, impel me, in view of the Gestapo's actions, to say this publicly.

Source J: from a letter sent by the Bishop of Limburg to the Minister of Justice, 13 August 1941.

Perhaps 8 km from Limburg, on a hill directly above the little town of Hadamar, there is an institution which used to serve a variety of purposes. Most recently it was a religious and nursing institution. It has been converted and kitted out as a place in which (according to popular opinion) euthanasia has been carried out systematically for months – since around February 1941. The fact is well known throughout the government district of Wiesbaden, because death certificates are sent from a registry in Hadamar-Mönchberg to the home districts concerned . . .

All God-fearing people feel this extermination of the helpless is an almighty crime. And if this is the same as saying that Germany cannot win the war if there is still a just God, then these statements are not caused by a lack of love for the Fatherland, but rather from deeply concerned frame of mind about our Volk. The population just cannot understand that systematic actions are being carried out which, according to section 211 of the statutory law book, are punishable by death. The authority of the government as a moral concept is suffering a dreadful trauma because of these events.

Source K: Bishop Wurm to the Head of Hitler's Chancellery, 20 December 1943.

In agreement with the judgement of all truly Christian people in Germany, I must state that we Christians feel this policy of destroying the Jews to be a grave wrong, and one which will have fearful consequences for the German people. To kill without the necessity of war, and without legal judgement, contravenes God's commands even when it has been ordered by authority, and, like every conscious violation of God's law, will be avenged, sooner or later.

Source L: from a sermon given by Bishop Galen in 1944.

In this hour I must direct a word of greeting and acknowledgement to our soldiers. I wish to express our gratitude to them for the loyal protection they have furnished the Fatherland and its borders at the price of unspeakable strains and sheer superhuman effort. In particular for the defence against the assaults of godless Bolshevism! And a word of deep-felt remembrance for those who, in the performance of their duty, have offered their lives and their last drop of blood for their brothers. May these all-sacrificing efforts succeed in winning for us an honourable and victorious peace!

Questions

1. Explain briefly the references to:
   (i) the 'sufferings of the Church' (Source H). [2]
   (ii) 'euthanasia' (Source J). [2]
2. According to Sources G, H, I, J and K, over what issues did the Catholic Church oppose government policies? [5]
3. What evidence is there in Sources F to L that the Catholic Church in Germany was 'patriotic'? [4]
*4. What other types of source would be of use to the historian investigating how widespread was opposition to Nazi policies from the Catholic Church? [4]
5. 'The opposition of Catholics to the Nazi regime steadily strengthened between 1933 and 1945.' Examine this view in the light of Sources F to L and of your own knowledge. [8]

Worked answer

*4. [This asks for types of source rather than specifically named sources. The important thing is to achieve a variety.]

All but one of the sources provided are of a single type: they are produced by Church leaders. A variety of other sources would be needed to supplement these, always supposing that these had survived destruction in the last stages of the war. One type would be the official responses of government departments to the complaints of Bishop Wurm, the Bishop of Limburg and Cardinal Galen. Another would be the parish records indicating church attendance: did this increase or decline during the Nazi era? A third would be the attitudes of other members of the clergy at different levels: how many other letters of complaint were sent to the departments, or letters of support to Galen? A fourth would be material linking the Catholic Church to political opposition or to the emergence of the Christian Democratic Union in the immediate postwar era. Finally, do the SOPADE reports contain any reference to Catholic dissidents? All of these would help to establish the extent of support for the initiatives of the few leaders shown in the Sources.

5

THE NAZI ECONOMY

BACKGROUND NARRATIVE

Hitler came to power after the worst of the Depression. Chancellor Brüning (1929–32) had introduced a series of deflationary measures which were intended to promote early recovery even at the expense of accelerating short-term economic decline. There is evidence that his policies were beginning to work: unemployment was already on the downturn and Hitler was able to claim the credit for the recovery.

The period 1933–6 was dominated by the Economics Minister, Hjalmar Schacht, whose New Plan of 1934 was intended to promote Germany's exports, reduce imports, strengthen the currency and establish a series of bilateral trade agreements with those less developed countries which were rich in raw materials. For a while therefore there was economic equilibrium. Between 1935 and 1936, however, an economic crisis forced Hitler to make a decision about future priorities. He therefore introduced in 1936 the Four Year Plan, the intention of which was to develop substitutes for essential raw materials which Germany lacked and to move to a war footing. The result was a rapid increase in the rate of rearmament. Military expenditure increased from 1.9 billion marks in 1933 to 5.8 billion at the start of the Four Year Plan, rising to 18.4 billion in 1938 and 32.3 billion in 1939. Accompanying rearmament was a series of measures to create a more disciplined workforce. In place of the trade unions, the workforce had to accept membership of organisations such as Strength through Joy (KdF) and Beauty of Labour (SDA) while, at the same time, coming to terms with falling living standards.

Two key issues arise from this outline. One is Hitler's overall economic strategy, the other the way in which this affected the German people.

ANALYSIS (1): HOW DID HITLER'S ECONOMIC POLICIES RELATE TO HIS SCHEMES FOR TERRITORIAL EXPANSION?

Hitler was not an economic theorist. Unlike Marxism, the ideology of Nazism had no underlying economic component: there was no equivalent to the notion of political change occurring through the dialectical conflict between classes exerting their economic interest. Nazism was fundamentally racist and *völkisch* in its conception, and economic factors were always subordinate. It would therefore be inappropriate to seek in it any autonomous economic strategy.

Nevertheless Hitler did have ideas which influenced his economic policy. These can be extracted from *Mein Kampf* and the *Zweites Buch*. Four main priorities can be deduced. First, Hitler aimed to create an autarkic system which would enable Germany to sustain a broader hegemony within Europe. He intended, second, to target above all the lands to the east. Third, since this inevitably involved expansion – and therefore conflict – the economic infrastructure would have to accommodate a considerable increase in military expenditure. But, fourth, he needed the support of the German people and could not therefore risk severely depressing their living standards in any quest for military supremacy. How did these components fit together? Broadly, the 1920s saw the emergence of Hitler's policy on *Lebensraum*, which was to provide the infrastructure for all of Hitler's ideas about the ultimate purpose of economic change. Then, after 1933, Hitler had the opportunity to implement these ideas. This is where explanations can be advanced which are so different as to be almost the reverse of each other.

Hitler's underlying economic approach emerged during the course of the 1920s. During this period there were two possible approaches to the establishment of future Nazi economic policy. One was socialism, which was strongest in the early 1920s. As we have seen in Chapter 1, this was championed by Gregor Strasser against the strong opposition of Hitler, who preferred the alternative to which he was becoming personally committed. This was a distinctively nationalist approach, based on the logical connection between territorial expansion and self-sufficiency: *Lebensraum* and autarky, the twin pillars of

Hitler's strategy, were developed in the second volume of *Mein Kampf*, published in 1925, and his *Zweites Buch*, written in 1928 but never published. In the former he argued that Germany should abandon its former pursuit of economic power through colonies or attempts to dominate western Europe and, instead, should be 'turning our eyes towards the land in the east. We are finally putting a stop to the colonial and trade policy of the pre-war period and passing over to the territorial policy of the future.'[1] Hence large peasant communities would eventually be established in the future in Poland and Russia on land carved out of these countries by the German army. German hegemony would also ensure self-sufficiency in all raw materials and food as well as guaranteed outlets for manufactured goods. Such goals would, of course, involve conflict, another key ingredient of Hitler's thinking. After all, Hitler said in a speech in 1923: 'It has ever been the right of the stronger . . . to see his will prevail.' Indeed, 'All of nature is one great struggle between strength and weakness, an eternal victory of the strong over the weak . . . The nation which would violate this elementary law would rot away.'[2]

These ideas have sometimes been dismissed as the vague fantasies of an immature fringe politician. This is a mistake, on two counts. First, there were many on the conservative right who took them seriously in the late 1920s and early 1930s because *Lebensraum* fitted closely into the pan-German concepts apparent in the Second Reich. Hitler therefore found ready converts among the so-called respectable sectors of big business, the armaments industry and the military high command. Many non-Nazis, in other words, recognised the flow of the argument and were certainly willing to take it seriously. Second, the eventual shaping of German hegemony in Europe bears a close resemblance to the original prototype, even if it was to be implemented by the SS rather than through Hitler's State channels. *Mein Kampf* need not be considered the 'blueprint' for Hitler's future projects, as suggested by Trevor-Roper, but it is surely more than the daydreaming attributed to it by A. J. P. Taylor.

Autarky would underpin the future economy; *Lebensraum* would give autarky geographical cohesion; and rearmament would provide the means of achieving *Lebensraum*. But how would this process actually be achieved? Two contrasting answers suggest themselves.

One line of argument would stress that the implementation of economic policy became essentially pragmatic. Hitler had to modify his theories on the domestic front, just as he did in his foreign policy, until he could be certain of his power base. The initial policies of Schacht, Hitler's Economics Minister, were therefore based on immediate requirements such as job-creation to reduce unemployment and wage controls to prevent the threat of inflation. Above all, Schacht followed the sensible course of establishing trade agreements with the Balkan states; these provided for the import of essential raw materials in exchange for credits on German industrial goods. Hitler tolerated Schacht until 1936, by which time he had come to place more emphasis on rearmament than Schacht thought wise. By now, Hitler reasoned, recovery from the depression had been sufficiently rapid to allow an acceleration of the rearmament policy: this was to be the key factor in the Four Year Plan (1936–40). In 1937 Hitler made clear his decision to prepare for war at the meeting with his chiefs of staff recorded in the Hossbach Memorandum. Hence Goering, at the Four Year Plan Office, was instructed to place the German economy on a war footing by promoting self-sufficiency and developing substitutes for any essential materials which Germany had to import.

Again, however, Hitler had to settle for a pragmatic course. Several historians have argued that he could not pursue a policy geared to total mobilisation and total war. Klein maintains that he still needed the support of the German consumer and therefore had to settle for a compromise – for an economy which would allow a limited degree of rearmament while, at the same time, allowing a reasonable level of consumer affluence.[3] According to Sauer, this balance meant the creation of a 'plunder economy'. The only way in which Germany could grow from limited mobilisation was by steadily expanding its economic base through a series of rapid and specifically targeted conquests. Hence Hitler 'committed himself to starting a war in the near future'.[4] The method used, *Blitzkrieg*, was as much an economic strategy as a military device. And it seemed to work. By 1941 *Blitzkrieg* seemed to have produced the required impetus for the achievement of the early stages of *Lebensraum*. Germany had gained military and economic control over Czechoslovakia, Poland, the Ukraine and a sizeable area of European Russia, as well as direct influence over Hungary, Romania and Bulgaria. With these victories, the economic dimension of *Lebensraum* became clearer. According to Hiden and Farquharson: 'the economic reorganization of Europe continued also to reflect the durability of National Socialist attempts to bring into being a viable alternative both to centralized state planning, as under Marxism, and to the liberal capitalist order which they had seen collapse in 1929.'[5] The former was repugnant on ideological grounds – especially since Nazism had abandoned the socialist elements of its early policy. The capitalist system was based on the sort of liberal principles which were incompatible with Nazi occupational policies. Hence the Nazis in implementing *Lebensraum* developed a policy of internal economic empire akin to the earlier European policy of mercantilism.

Then came total war, which wrecked the new economic order. Total war is often projected as the logical final step: the total mobilisation of the economy to enable it to achieve the final stage. Actually, it was a response to failure to achieve a further rapid victory through *Blitzkrieg*. It was an admission that the previous delicate balance between consumer and military needs could no longer be maintained. Above all, it was a struggle for survival as, from 1942 onwards, the tide began to turn with the military recovery of the Soviet Union and the entry of the United States into the war. Despite the best efforts of Armaments Minister, Albert Speer, the German economy proved far less adaptable to total war than those of its three main rivals. It was massively outproduced in terms of war material by the United States and Soviet Union, while even Britain, with a smaller, economic base, managed to maintain a larger per capita output of aircraft and artillery. It seems, therefore, that total war was a desperate attempt to cling on to the *Lebensraum* already achieved rather than its logical completion.

This is one view of the relationship between *Blitzkrieg* and total war. It is, however, possible to put forward an entirely different scenario. From the start, Hitler moved systematically towards equipping Germany with an economic base capable of achieving *Lebensraum*. According to Berghahn, 'the rearmament programme which was begun in 1933 amounted . . . to nothing less than a deliberate unhinging of the national economy with the intention of recovering the financial losses by exploiting other national economies of Europe within the confines of German-dominated empire conquered by force'.[6] It is true that some of Schacht's policies were a continuation of the deflationary approach of Bruning. They were, however, tolerated by Hitler who saw them as essential for the establishment of the infrastructure of autarky. Hence the trading networks with the Balkans would become the first step in the establishment of German hegemony; the public works schemes, especially for the *Autobahns*, would help create a military infrastructure; and the controls on wages would create a disciplined workforce which would become increasingly receptive to intensive mobilisation. Hitler was therefore using Schacht's New Plan as the first stage in the move towards total war.

But the process was not to be so easy. Hitler's hand was forced by a major economic crisis between 1935 and 1936 in the form of a food shortage affecting the whole of the German workforce. He took what he considered to be the only way out: to impose further constraints on the workforce while, at the same time, accelerating rearmament to achieve *Lebensraum* and autarky. The whole purpose of the Four Year Plan was therefore to prepare for war; this became clear in the Hossbach Memorandum, which anticipated that 'Our relative strength would decrease in relation to the rearmament which would by then have been carried out by the rest of the world. If we did not act by 1943–45, any year would, owing to a lack of reserves, produce the food crisis, to cope with which the necessary foreign exchange was not available.'[7] It seems logical, therefore, that Hitler was gearing the German economy to the total war which would be necessary in order to achieve the *Lebensraum* which would be its long-term economic salvation.

There were, however, to be complications. The outbreak of war with Britain and France in 1939 was premature, which meant that the economy could support only *Blitzkrieg* military strategies. *Blitzkrieg* was therefore an emergency response – or, in the words of Overy, 'total war by default'.[8] It was not until 1941 that the economy of Germany had been sufficiently enlarged to move to a full-scale mobilisation of resources – the whole point of total war. But total war now went on to produce defeat rather than victory. This was because of the original mistiming of *Blitzkrieg*, which had prevented a proper buildup of resources, and the subsequent involvement of the United States, which meant the dissipation of those resources in a conflict on two fronts. Hence the total-war economy failed not because it was the reversal of a successful phase of *Blitzkrieg*, but because it was rendered incomplete by *Blitzkrieg* as an unnecessary diversion. Overy's view is therefore the reverse of that of Sauer and Klein. He argues that 'If war had been postponed until 1943–5 as Hitler had hoped, then Germany would have been much better prepared, and would also have had rockets, inter-continental bombers, perhaps even atomic weapons. Though Britain and France did not know it, declaring war in 1939 prevented Germany from becoming the super-power Hitler wanted.'[9]

For once, it is genuinely difficult to synthesise what appear to be two mutually exclusive interpretations. Either the *Blitzkrieg* economy was the initially successful step towards *Lebensraum* which was then reversed by the disasters of total war. Or the drive for *Lebensraum* through total war was impeded by the intrusion of *Blitzkrieg*. Either is possible but, pending further research, the verdict should perhaps remain open.

Questions

1. What was the relationship between 'autarky' and 'Leben-sraum' in Nazi economic theory?
2. In economic terms, was 'total war' the logical outcome outcome of 'Blitzkrieg'?

ANALYSIS (2): DO THE STATISTICS SHOW THAT THE GERMAN PEOPLE WERE BETTER OFF AS A RESULT OF HITLER'S ECONOMIC POLICIES?

In 1938 a Cambridge economics lecturer wrote after a visit to Germany: 'No-one who is acquainted with German conditions would suggest that the standard of living is a high one, but the important thing is that it has been rising in recent years.'[10] At a superficial level this statement can be supported by statistics of the period. More detailed analysis, however, shows a different picture: that, in relative terms, the standard of living was at best static and, by some criteria, actually deteriorating.

There seemed to be much to support the view that Germany was experiencing a return to prosperity after the trauma of the Depression. For one thing, unemployment was in rapid decline. The figure had stood at 4.8 million in 1933, dropping thereafter to 2.7 million in 1934, 2.2 million in 1935, 1.6 million in 1936, 0.9 million in 1937, 0.4 million in 1938 and a mere 0.1 million by 1939.[11] This was far more rapid than the reduction of unemployment in comparable economies such as the United States and France, while Britain still had 1.8 million on the dole in 1938. Corresponding with the decline in unemployment was an increase in wages. Falling to a low in 1933 of 70 per cent of their 1928 level, these had recovered to 75 per cent by 1934, 80 per cent by 1936 and 85 per cent by 1938.

Thus by a double criterion more and more people became better and better off during the six years after 1933. They were also part of a general increase in prosperity represented by a steady growth of Germany's national income from 44 billion marks in 1933 to 80 billion in 1938. This was particularly impressive since the 1938 figure was actually greater than the 72 billion of 1928, despite the fall in the value of the mark in the meantime. The workforce benefited at certain key outlets within the economy as the production of some consumer goods seemed to take off. Germans, for example, became the world's largest per-capita owners of radio sets, while progress was also made in developing the comparatively cheap Volkswagen car. Added to these benefits was the vast range of activities provided in Strength through Joy (KdF): these included concerts, operas, theatre, cabaret, films, guided tours, sporting events and gymnastics, cruises and hikes. Meanwhile, Beauty of Labour (SDA) did much to improve working conditions, reduce problems such as noise levels and increase co-operation and solidarity in the workplace. Certainly the workforce as a whole was far better off than that in the Soviet Union. It was not, by and large, in constant dread of being denounced to the Gestapo or being forced to reach unrealistic targets by being driven to breaking point. Overall, it is easy to see why contemporaries should have seen Nazi Germany as a country undergoing a transformation in its economy to the ultimate benefit of its people.

There are, however, fundamental problems with this line of reasoning. Its underlying assumption is that any improvements after 1933 were due directly and solely to Hitler's policies. But this is flawed, on two counts. First, there is more continuity between the early policies of the Third Reich and the later policies of the Weimar Republic than is often realised. In economic terms, the dividing line is really in 1929. There was far more difference between the policies of Müller and Brüning than between those of Papen or Schleicher and Hitler. Second, the policy of Brüning created a dynamic which was of double benefit to Hitler. In ruthlessly taking control of the economy, Brüning intended to deal forcefully with the problems as quickly as possible in order to enable Germany to come through the other side of the economic crisis more quickly than any of the other leading industrial powers. This benefited Hitler's reputation by creating a huge peak of unemployment which Hitler could not help but alleviate. And, by the time that Hitler had come to power, the worse was over as Brüning's policies were beginning to have an admittedly belated impact. In other words, Hitler inherited a disastrous situation which was just about on the mend.

Even so, the improvement which did occur was not fully transmitted to the workforce, since it was not consumer-based. The focus of the economy was switched, especially from 1936, to rearmament and an expansion in the size of the armed forces. Declining unemployment was, it could be said, artificially induced. This was also apparent in the calculated use of the unemployed on public works schemes such as the construction of *Autobahns*. Such expedients are rarely possible within a democracy since they remove the element of choice from unemployment. It might be argued that the unemployed have no choice, but it is important for the government of a democratic regime to assume that they do, so that it will place solutions on persuasion rather than coercion. This was certainly the case with Roosevelt's New Deal. On the other hand, a totalitarian regime can dispense altogether with the very notion of choice and, through coercive measures, generate an immediate impact on unemployment levels. As Germany accelerated the pace of rearmament through the Four Year Plan, unemployment levels were bound to drop like a stone.

The counterpart to forced employment was a disciplined workforce held to lower wage levels. Pay may have increased relative to the year 1933 but there was no return to 1928: indeed the percentages for 1933 and 1939 were 77 per cent and 89 per cent respectively.[12] This was hardly a massive upswing. Besides, the wage earner was actually worse off in terms of the cost of living. This had increased from 71 per cent of the 1928 level in 1932 to 90 per cent in 1939. In real terms, therefore, those in employment had been marginally better off in 1933 than they were in 1939. The workforce received an ever declining proportion of the national income as wages. In 1933, for example, wages amounted to 63 per cent of the national income, while by 1938 they had dropped steadily each year to 57 per cent. It is also significant that these wages were earned through a working week which had been extended on average by over seven hours.

Declining wages were accompanied by reduced attention to consumer needs. It is true that between 1933 and 1938 the level of consumer goods rose by 69 per cent. But, over the same period, industrial goods increased by 389 per cent. In other words, workers were producing proportionately more in terms of heavy industrial goods and armaments than they were consumables. It can also be deduced from import and export figures that the general flow of trade was not in the consumers' interest. Imports in 1932 totalled 4.6 billion marks, compared with 5.7 billion marks for exports. The corresponding figures for 1930 had been 12.4 billion and 12.0 billion. The consumer suffered in two ways – the imposition of tight import controls by Schacht and the huge drop in consumer goods from abroad.[13]

As to the new employee organisations, these may have had certain benefits and attractions, but they were very much in line with the aims of a totalitarian regime. The workforce was strictly regulated even down to its use of free time. This was done partly to break any desire to revive consumer habits, which would draw off resources from rearmament, and partly to keep open the channels of propaganda and indoctrination. The KdF and SDA were therefore no substitute for the trade unionism which had been banned by Hitler in 1933. Free collective bargaining, which had been such a prominent feature of the Weimar Republic, had been replaced by the creation of corporate identity and interest. It is true that it lacked the crude terror of the Soviet system, but it was no less pervasive in its destruction of individual values. Exploitation was as much a feature of the Nazi economy as of its Soviet counterpart – even if in Germany the stick was disguised as the carrot.

In reality, therefore, the German workforce was putting in longer hours for a fractional notional increase in wages. In real terms wages were actually in decline compared to the increase in the standard of living. The input that workers had into the economy was substantial but largely one-way: it fed into rearmament but received few consumables in exchange. Returning to the opening quotation, therefore, it now seems that the standard of living was falling, not rising.

Questions

1. Was the Cambridge economics lecturer, referred to in Analysis (2), correct?
2. Was the German workforce exploited by the Nazi regime?

SOURCES

1. STATISTICS OF THE GERMAN ECONOMY

Source A: unemployment figures 1928–39.

	No. (000s)	% of working population
1928	1,391	6.3
1929	1,899	8.5
1930	3,076	14.0
1931	4,520	21.9
1932	5,603	29.9
1933	4,804	25.9
1934	2,718	13.5
1935	2,151	10.3
1936	1,593	7.4
1937	912	4.1
1938	429	1.9
1939	119	0.5

Source B: imports and exports 1925–35 (million marks, current prices).

	Exports	Imports
1925	9,284	12,429
1930	12,036	10,349
1932	5,741	4,653

Source C: index of wages (1936 = 100).

	Comparison with 1936
1928	125
1933	88
1934	94
1936	100
1938	106

Source D: national income (million marks).

1928	72,000
1932	43,000
1933	44,000
1936	64,000
1938	80,000

Source E: wages as a percentage of national income.

1928	62
1932	64
1933	63
1934	62
1936	59
1938	57

Source F: index of industrial and consumer goods (1928 = 100).

	Industrial goods	Consumer goods
1928	100	100
1933	56	80
1934	81	91
1936	114	100
1938	144	116

Source G: Comparative military expenditure: Germany and Britain (% of GNP).

	Germany	Britain
1935	8	2
1936	13	5
1937	13	7
1938	17	8
1939	23	22
1940	38	53
1941	47	60
1942	55	64
1943	61	63

Questions

1. Why did unemployment go down, as shown in Source A, between 1933 and 1939? [4]
2. How would you explain the apparent variation in the figures in Source B? [3]
3. Do sources C, D, E and F show that the German consumer prospered under Nazi rule? [4]
*4. Comment on the comparisons shown in Source G between the military expenditures of Germany and Britain. [6]
5. How much did the economic policy of the Nazi regime have in mind the needs of the German consumer? Base your answer on the sources and your own knowledge. [8]

Worked answer

*4. ['Comment on' means more than 'describe'. The answer to this question should therefore include a comparison between the trends shown by the figures *and* attempt an explanation for the difference between them.]

The figures in Source G show a clear difference in the overall trends of German and British military expenditure. Germany's expenditure rose sharply in 1936, with a further increase between 1938 and 1939. British expenditure, in proportion to GNP, was substantially slower in its increase but had virtually caught up by 1939. Thereafter, both countries allocated a higher proportion of their GNP to pursuing the war, but the British involvement seems to have been more intensive in 1941 and 1942.

This pattern ties in with Germany's preparation for a limited war, or *Blitzkrieg*, envisaged by the Four Year Plan from 1936. The intention was that this should continue with the invasion of Russia. However, the military problems encountered meant that Germany had to mobilise from 1942 for 'total war' – hence the sharp increase in military expenditure. Britain, by contrast, went straight to preparedness for total war and, between 1940 and 1943, managed to mobilise a larger proportion of its resources; this implies a slower start but a higher eventual level of efficiency.

SOURCES

2. THE FOUR YEAR PLAN

Source H: extracts from Hitler's announcement of the Four Year Plan (1936).

Politics are the conduct and the course of the historical struggle of nations for life. The aim of these struggles is survival ... No nation will be able to avoid or abstain from this historical conflict ...

Germany's economic situation is ... in the briefest outline as follows:
1. We are overpopulated and cannot feed ourselves from our own resources ...
6. The final solution lies in extending our living space, that is to say, extending the sources of raw materials and foodstuffs of our people. It is the task of the political leadership one day to solve this problem ...

I thus set the following tasks:

I. The German armed forces must be operational within four years.
II. The German economy must be fit for war within four years.

Source I: Schacht's comment, written in his autobiography in 1949, on the management of the Four Year Plan by Goering.

Goering set out, with all the folly and incompetence of the amateur, to carry out the programme of economic self-sufficiency, or autarky, envisaged in the Four Year Plan. Hitler had made him chief of the Four Year Plan operations in order to extend his own influence over economic policy, which he did not find difficult, since he was now, of course, in a position to place really large contracts . . . On December 17th 1936, Goering informed a meeting of big industrialists that it was no longer a question of producing economically, but simply of producing. And as far as getting hold of foreign exchange was concerned it was quite immaterial whether the provisions of the law were complied with or not . . . Goering's policy of recklessly exploiting Germany's economic substance necessarily brought me into more and more open conflict with him, and for his part he exploited his powers, with Hitler and the Party behind him, to counter my activity as Minister of Economics to an ever-increasing extent.

Source J: from a speech given by Goering to German industrialists on 17 December 1936.

The context to which we look forward calls for enormous efficiency. No end to rearmament is in sight. All that matters is victory or defeat. If we conquer, the business world will be fully indemnified. We must not reckon profit and loss according to the book, but only according to political needs. There must be no calculations of cost. I require you to do all you can and to prove that part of the national fortune is in your hands. Whether new investment can be written off in every case is a matter of indifference. We are playing for the highest stakes. What can be more profitable than rearmament orders?

Source K: from an analysis in a report produced by SOPADE (the Social Democratic Party in exile).

The Nazis try to persuade the nation that the problem of economic constraints is nothing but a foreign exchange problem, whereas in reality it is a problem of the capacity of the economy and of the nation's willingness to make sacrifices. This problem has two aspects: on the one hand, the problem of economic resources, of the maximum level of production and the minimum level of consumption; and, on the other hand, the problem of money, of the financial constraints. What the superficial observer normally notices, however, is the constricting effect of the foreign exchange shortage with which Germany continually has to cope . . .

If, in contrast to the foreign trade of America and Britain and that of other industrial countries, German foreign trade cannot recover, the cause lies primarily in the enormous demands placed on the German economy by rearmament ... If production geared to rearmament and the autarky programme is set against the production for export and consumption (including production geared to the expansion of the consumer goods industries), it is clear that the one can grow only at the expense of the other ...

The shortage of foreign exchange is, therefore, in reality only a reflection of the overloading of Germany's economic strength through rearmament and the autarky programme.

Source L: Production of key commodities, as compared with the target of the Four Year Plan (thousand tons).

	1936	1938	1942	Plan target
Mineral oil	1,790	2,340	6,260	13,830
Rubber	0.7	5	96	120
Explosives	18	45	300	223
Steel	19,216	22,656	20,800	24,000
Coal	319,782	381,171	411,977	453,500

Questions

1. (i) Who were Schacht and Goering (Sources I and J)? [2]
    (ii) What is meant by 'autarky' (Source K)? [1]
2. How much light does Source J throw on Source K? [4]
*3. What are the comparative advantages and disadvantages of Sources I and K to the historian studying the Four Year Plan? [5]
4. To what extent can Source H be considered to have been fulfilled by Source L? [5]
5. 'The Four Year Plan was designed to break normal economic relations with other states and to create an economy geared to plunder.' Do these sources, and your own knowledge, support this view? [8]

Worked answer

*3. [This questions requires comments on the nature and content of the two sources, written within the context of an overall comparison between the two.]

A number of advantages and disadvantages emerge from a comparison of Sources I and K. First, in terms of personal involvement and imme-diate knowledge, Source K seems to have the main advantage, since Schacht was Reich Finance Minister between 1933 and 1937. The Social Democratic Party, by contrast, had never had any role in the German economy after 1933 and could be seen to have lost all contact while in exile. Second, in terms of detachment, however, Source I has an obvious disadvantage: Schacht bitterly resented his replace-ment by Goering in 1937 and his description of the latter's 'folly and incompetence' was clearly personally motivated. Source K keeps personalities out of the picture, concentrating on gathering information for use in an assessment of how to oppose the regime. Third, the date of publication is significant. Source I, published in 1949, has the advantage of longer-term perspective but the disadvantage of Schacht's obvious desire to distance himself from the policies of a defeated and discredited regime. Source I has a more immediate view, which is not informed about the future. Finally, there is a clear contrast in terms of content. The focus of Source I is stronger on the imple-mentation of the Plan than on its principles, while Source K shows the reverse. In this respect, the two Sources are most useful when taken in conjunction.

6

RACE, THE HOLOCAUST AND THE JEWISH RESPONSE

BACKGROUND NARRATIVE

The Nazi regime was totally committed to the pursuit of a racial policy of Aryanism, or the projection of the German people as the master race. This involved the concept of Social Darwinism, or the survival of the fittest. Analysis (1) shows the origins and importance of this, along with the implications for those who were genetically 'impaired' in any way. Compulsory sterilisation was introduced for the latter in 1933, the scope eventually being extended to include 'community aliens' such as tramps, homosexuals and gypsies. From 1939 the regime went further still with a 'euthanasia' programme to destroy Germany's mentally ill patients.

The most extreme part of the racialist policy was the persecution of the Jews. Anti-semitism had existed in Germany, as in the rest of Europe, for many centuries but, after Hitler's rise to power, was officially enshrined in Nazi policy and legislation. The process started with a boycott of Jewish shops by the SA in April 1933. In the same month Jews were dismissed from the civil service and, in September 1933, were prevented from inheriting land. Further constraints were placed in 1935 on their use of parks, swimming baths and public buildings, while in the same year the Nuremberg Laws banned any marriage or sexual intercourse between Jews and non-Jews. There was also a considerable amount of anti-Jewish propaganda, which poured out of the anti-semitic press. The situation seemed to improve for a while with the removal of discriminatory signs during the 1936 Berlin Olympics, but then took a sharp turn for the worse in 1938 on Kristallnacht, an orgy of destruction directed against Jewish shops and synagogues. From this point onwards the state began to identify Jews more explicitly. In 1938 they were permitted to use only authorised Jewish names and, from 1941, were obliged to wear the Star of David.

The whole process was radicalised by the war. From 1941 onwards the 'Final Solution' killed over six million Jews in new extermination camps set up in occupied Poland: these were Auschwitz, Treblinka, Maidanek, Sobibor and Chelmo. The origins of this genocide are dealt with in Analysis (2). It is often said that the Jewish population of Germany and the occupied territories did little to resist these measures; this is examined in Analysis (3).

ANALYSIS (1): WHAT ROLE DID RACE PLAY IN THE NAZI SYSTEM?

Race is usually seen as the most illogical component of the entire Nazi system, the one which made it a totalitarian regime capable of committing acts of great evil. This is, of course, the truth – but not the whole truth. Race was also the fundamental rationale for all social developments: indeed, race and society were inseparable.

The foundation of the Nazi race doctrine was the concept of genetic drive. This was rooted in nineteenth-century ideas of fringe theorists such as Gobineau, Houston and Chamberlain. Collectively known as Social Darwinists, they transferred the scientific concept of the survival of the fittest from the animal to the human world. In 1915 the biologist Haeckel argued that 'the theory of selection teaches us that organic progress is an inevitable consequence of the struggle for existence'.[1] Hitler took this a stage further and based his whole ideology on the premise of struggle, which he saw as 'the father of all things'. From this emerged the right of the strong to triumph over the weak. Indeed, this was essential, since the strong created, while the weak are undermined and destroyed. He emphasised that 'All the human culture, all the results of art, science and technology that we see before us today, are almost exclusively the creative product of the Aryan.'[2] Conversely, 'All the great cultures of the past were destroyed only because the originally creative race died from blood poisoning.' The solution was obvious. 'Therefore, he who would live, let him fight, and he who would not fight in this world of struggle is not deserving of life.'[3]

The implications of this theoretical framework were huge. Race, linked to struggle, provided a new approach to the organic development of the Nazi society and State. In this respect Nazism was as utopian and revolutionary as communism, since it aimed at nothing less than total transformation. The racial doctrine had three dimensions: it provided Germany with its purpose, its cohesion – and its victims.

The ultimate purpose of the Nazi system was to transcend the existing limits of the State. Here we can see a contrast with fascist Italy. Mussolini saw the highest political form as the nation state, which he sought to extend into a revived form of the Roman Empire. This expansion of the étatist core into a larger imperium was both historical and traditional in its concept. In the case of Nazi Germany, étatism was not the main priority: this was the *Volksgemeinschaft*, or the 'people's community', which was to be the higher form of the State. Similarly, the focus of German expansion was not the establishment of a traditional empire, but rather to provide 'our nation with sufficient living space. Such living space can only be in the east.'[4] Unlike Mussolini, Hitler's emphasis was not imperial, but *völkisch*. Étatism, for Italy the main aim, was, for Nazi Germany, merely the first step to Aryanism and *Lebensraum*. The driving force for this was the concept of the master race.

Racial theory also aimed at creating a new form of social cohesion – by replacing class divisions with racial unity and racial supremacy. The *Volksgemeinschaft* would reconcile what Peukert calls a 'society of fractured traditions, social classes and environments'.[5] In place of embittered Germans from competing economic groups, there would emerge healthy, vigorous and productive Aryans. The new stereotype proved attractive to most of the population and therefore ensured their loyalty to a regime which appeared to value them so highly. This, of course, was part of the overall formula. For, in return for their new unity of purpose and elevated status, the people were to be 'primed for self-sacrifice'.[6] Hence the racial policies were closely connected not only with the propaganda and indoctrination trends within Germany's schools (see Chapter 3) but also with the new work ethic implicit in organisations like the Reich Labour Service (RAD), SDA and KdF. According to Peukert, racialism was 'a reflection of welfare workers' everyday experience and problems, to which a racialist solution seemed to be the obvious one'.[7]

To be fully effective the *Volksgemeinschaft* needed to have its 'impurities' removed. The victims were all those who, for genetic reasons, did not fit into the stereotype of Aryanism. This might be for reasons of ethnic origins, physical or mental impairment, or social deviance: hence the concept of racial purity therefore had several forms of inward focus. Those suffering from hereditary diseases were compulsorily sterilised from 1933 as a result of the Law for the Prevention of the Hereditarily Diseased. Between 1934 and 1939 this affected some 0.5 per cent of the entire population. From 1939 the scope was extended through the introduction of the euthanasia programme: between 1939 and 1941 about 72,000 people were killed in this way. To these can be added large numbers of tramps, vagrants, alcoholics and homosexuals. These were all considered 'alien to the community' (*gemeinschaftsfremd*) and had therefore become race enemies in the broader sense. The *Volksgemeinschaft* therefore achieved cohesion by replacing class conflict with targeted persecution. 'Thus', argues Schoenbaum, 'Nazi social theory denied equality while at the same time asserting it.'[8]

The largest single group of victims was the Jews. Their persecution provided the regime with its dynamic and with the primitive elements of vicious hatred. In part, German anti-semitism was the culmination of centuries of discrimination throughout Europe: this had reared its head again after 1880, with violence in Vienna and Berlin, blatant discrimination in the French army and a series of pogroms in Tsarist Russia. H. S. Chamberlain justified such events within the context of tradition. He wrote in 1901: 'The entrance of the Jew into European History had meant the entrance of an alien element – alien to that which Europe had already achieved, alien to all it was still destined to achieve.'[9] Anti-semitism could therefore be seen as a tidal force: its high-water mark at the turn of the nineteenth century brought Hitler in with its flotsam.

Hitler's own views on Jews were the main driving force behind the whole Nazi ideology and movement; anti-semitic policies were therefore a sublimation of his personal obsession. *Mein Kampf* and his speeches are full of the most inflammatory references. In the former he created the stereotype of the Jew as a parasite and pollutant: 'Culturally he contaminates art, literature and the theatre, makes a mockery of national feeling, overthrows all concepts of beauty, and instead drags men down into the sphere of his own base nature.'[10] In one of his speeches he fantasised about hanging the Jews of Munich from lamp posts until their 'bodies rotted'. There is no doubting the elemental force of his hatred. At the same time, there was also a deliberately pragmatic use of the techniques of scapegoating: the paradox was that anti-semitism as an irrational force could be used rationally to strengthen the *Volksgemeinschaft*. This worked as follows. There would be numerous occasions on which the regime called for sacrifice. This would elicit two sentiments: a positive effort and negative feelings of resentment at the sacrifice required. The former would be used by the regime, but the latter needed to be deflected away from the regime. For the mentality attuned to Social Darwinism it made sense to target a minority group which had been picked out by the Führer from the taint of many centuries. The methods used to generate hatred were varied. One was the spread of the vilest misinformation, based on Hitler's earlier principle of the 'big lie'. Hence, Streicher's newspaper *Der Stürmer* alleged ritual killing of Christian children by Jews. 'The blood of the victims is to be forcibly tapped . . . the fresh (or powdered) blood of the slaughtered child is further used by young married Jewish couples, by pregnant Jewesses, for circum- cision and so forth.'[11] Another was Hitler's oratorical device of blaming Jews for all perceived threats, ranging from the economic crisis of 1935–6 to the hostility of Britain and France to German designs on Poland in 1939. A third was the carefully orchestrated 'spontaneity' of Kristallnacht, publicised by Goebbels as the expression of the 'righteous indignation of the German people'.

In summary, Nazi race policy did three things. First, it converted traditional étatism into a more radical Aryanism, the ultimate thrust of which was *Lebensraum*. Second, it substituted for the older class divisions of German society the new unity of the *Volksgemeinschaft*. And, third, this unity was maintained at the expense of minorities which had no place within it. Some, the 'community aliens', were removed with as little fuss as possible. Others, especially the Jews, were deliberately set up as targets for any resentment which might be felt by members of the *Volksgemeinschaft* at the extent of the sacrifice demanded of them. Anti-semitism was the obvious vehicle for this, since it had deep historic roots and seemed to fit into the Führer's messianic claims. During the period 1933–41, therefore, racism and anti-semitism were widely accepted, although few could have predicted their eventual outcome.

Questions

1. Was race fundamental to Nazi theory?
2. What was the connection between race and the *Volksgemeinschaft*?

ANALYSIS (2): WHAT WAS THE GENESIS OF THE HOLOCAUST?

No historical topic is immune to controversy. Even the Holocaust, perhaps the most cataclysmic event in history, has produced polarised views. There are broadly speaking three debates. The first is whether it actually happened. This can be dismissed quickly. The vast majority of historians accept that the evidence for the Holocaust is over-whelming. A small minority, most prominently Irving, consider that the gas chambers were the creation of Allied propaganda in 1945; these, however, are pursuing an openly polemical line in support of the neo-Nazi cause and have thereby discredited themselves as serious historians. The second controversy is a more genuine one. Was the Holocaust the logical fulfilment of the Nazi policy of anti-semitism? Or is there more in the argument that the Holocaust was the result not of careful planning but rather of the failure of alternative strategies? The third debate concerns the extent of complicity: how much was the German population involved in the Holocaust and how was it possible for such actions to happen at all?

In considering whether the extermination of the Jews was always intended, or whether it emerged institutionally, few historians have seriously attempted to deny the ultimate responsibility of Hitler. The disagreement between them has arisen over the means by which his anti-semitism was converted into the 'Final Solution'.

One school, labelled the 'intentionalists', attributes the policy of genocide to the Führer state as a function of a personalised totalitarian regime. Historians who follow this line include Fleming, Jäckel and Hillgruber. They maintain that Hitler implemented the decision in the summer of 1941. The reason was that the collapse of Russia in the wake of the German invasion seemed inevitable and this was the perfect chance to achieve a long-held ambition. Goering therefore ordered Heydrich to bring about 'a complete solution of the Jewish question within the German sphere of influence in Europe'. Although no document has ever been found linking this order directly to Hitler, it makes no logical sense to deny his ultimate authorship. Dawidowicz places this in a more general context: she argues that there was a gradual escalation of persecution from the nineteenth century, through to Hitler's ideas in the 1920s, then to implementation in the 1930s, and ultimately to extermination. Most recently – and forcefully – Goldhagen has argued that there are four clear precursors in Hitler's thought and speeches for the Holocaust. First, 'Hitler expressed his obsessive eliminationist racist antisemitism from his earliest days in public life': this can be seen explicitly in *Mein Kampf*. Then, on coming to power,

Hitler 'turned the eliminationist antisemitism into unprecedented radical measures'. Third, in 1939 he 'repeated many times his prophecy, indeed his promise: the war would provide him with the opportunity to exterminate European Jewry'. This, finally, he proceeded to do 'when the moment was ripe'. Hence, Goldhagen concludes, 'The genocide was the outgrowth not of Hitler's moods, not of local initiative, not of the impersonal hand of structural obstacles, but of Hitler's ideal to eliminate all Jewish power.'[12]

There is, alternatively, a strong 'functionalist' argument that the extermination was a process which was arrived at as a logical sequence of administrative actions rather than as a preconceived plan. This view was pioneered by Hilberg as early as 1961.[13] It was subsequently continued – and refined – by Mommsen and Broszat. The basic argument is that the 'Final Solution' was not the solution originally intended but rather that arrived at because of the failure of all the others. It was the result of growing incompetence, not increased efficiency. The original target had been resettlement, first to Madagascar, then to Siberia. The former had been made impractical by the outbreak of war, which had focused Germany's priorities on Europe itself. The latter was impeded by the nature of the war against Russia. Proposals to transport all Jews over the Urals were set in motion but were then blocked by the revival of Russian resistance to the German advance. This meant an accumulation of peoples in eastern Europe with no obvious long-term destination in view. The result was the search for a swift solution, first through the SS *Einsatzgruppen* killings, then through the use of extermination camps.

This debate fits into the broader one of the nature of the Nazi State. It is no coincidence that the intentionalists also argue that the structure of dictatorship in Germany depended on the personality of Hitler himself and that he deliberately exploited any weaknesses and contradictions within it to his own advantage; this has already been discussed in Chapter 2. He would therefore have chosen the time, the method and the institutions for the implementation of a scheme of extermination which had always existed in his mind. The functionalists, by contrast, see consistency in the weakness of Hitler's response to institutional chaos and the disorganised way in which the Holocaust was finally implemented. This makes it possible to conclude that the Holocaust was the administrative response to the failure of earlier policies.

A possible synthesis may be that, while he was out of power, Hitler initially thought in terms of genocide – but then moderated this in order to broaden his support once he was in power. This explains why he limited early measures to the Nuremberg Laws and ordered the removal of discriminatory public notices at the time of the 1936 Berlin Olympics. It is true that there was a violent acceleration on Kristallnacht (1938). Nevertheless, there was no inexorable move towards extermination. Furthermore, during the first two years of the war, Hitler hoped for a possible peace with Britain and did not at this stage wish to antagonise the United States. The reaction of public opinion in these countries to genocide would have been one of horror, compared to the apparent indifference which had previously prevailed over earlier anti-semitic policies.[14]

But total war changed the whole situation. This occurred for two reasons. First, in invading the Soviet Union, Hitler was signalling that he considered that Britain was no longer capable of exerting any real threat: that Britain was now marginalised and therefore irrelevant. Germany could now focus on the racial struggle which Hitler had always foreseen. The defeat of the Soviet Union could now be accompanied by the removal of Jewry – by whatever method. But, with the failure to inflict permanent defeat on Russia in 1941, the struggle for racial conquest became one for racial survival – in which Hitler's ideas of extermination, already strongly hinted at, were crucial. The pursuit of total war against the Soviet Union required the total removal of the perceived racial enemy within. The belief that this internal enemy had always had strong connections with Soviet Marxism made the 'Final Solution' the more obvious. So far the impetus for genocide must be considered Hitler's. But the means by which this would be carried out resided with the SS, which alone could provide the degree of organisation and commitment that was needed. This returns to the theme of Chapter 4 that, by the time of the Second World War, the Nazi State had been largely superseded by the SS State.

The debate on the origins of the Holocaust also raises the question of the complicity of the German people.

The original interpretation places the focus on Hitler and his immediate henchmen, largely within the SS. In support of this, it can be argued that much of the population were held in the grip of a dictatorship which had two advantages over it. One was the regime's absolute control over information, the other the capacity to intimidate and terrorise. It is highly significant that both processes were under the control of one institution – the SS. Himmler gave explicit instructions for secrecy: he said of the extermination to an assembly of SS officials in Posen in 1943, 'Among ourselves, we can talk openly about it, though we can never speak a word of it in public.' He added, 'That is a page of glory in our history that never has been and never can be written.'[15] There was therefore a huge barrier of credibility: the idea of genocide was to most people unimaginable. And, if it was denied by the regime, why should rumours to the contrary be believed? Besides, if rumour-mongers were disposed of by the SS, this did not necessarily mean that the rumours were true: the use of terror had long been institutionalised for any form of dissent. How, therefore, could the German people reasonably have been expected to know what was going on?

The revised view spreads the degree of involvement and responsibility. Dülffer's view is typical. He argues that the Holocaust was above all due to Hitler. 'But to recognize this is not to exculpate the hundreds of thousands of others who were involved in carrying out the Final Solution.'[16] Goldhagen goes further. Hitler's ideal, he says, was 'broadly shared in Germany'.[17] This can be seen in several ways. The bureaucracy was involved on a huge scale and there was massive collaboration between the SS, the civil service, business corporations and the army. This deprived Jews of their rights and assets, isolated them, deported them and killed them. The army, too, was heavily implicated. In many cases the Wehrmacht actively co-operated with the SS – in contrast, it has to be said, with officers in the Italian army who officially protested against the killing of Italian Jews. The true extent of knowledge about and acceptance of the Holocaust will probably never now be known. But it is undoubtedly wider than was once believed.

This raises the disturbing question of how so many people could allow themselves to be involved in acts of evil. There can be no question that the participants were unaware of the real nature of what they were doing, whether in the *Einsatzgruppen* or in the camps. Even Rudolf Hoess, the commandant of Auschwitz, maintained that 'Our system is so terrible that no-one in the world will believe it to be possible.'[18] But how could this 'terrible system' have had so many practitioners? One possibility is that a minority of sadists enforced a system from which others knowingly followed through fear of retribution consequent on disobeying orders. The impetus here is evil as an active force, released by psychopathic behaviour. The main example would be the influence of Streicher, who derived sexual gratification from the persecution and torture of helpless people. There is no doubt that thousands of similar characters were attracted to membership of the SS by similar prospects. But it is equally certain that they were a small minority among all those involved in the Holocaust. There must be a better explanation.

The alternative, according to Hannah Arendt, is that the process of extermination was dealt with 'neither by fanatics nor by natural murderers nor by sadists. It was manned solely and exclusively by normal human beings of the type of Heinrich Himmler.'[19] Far from being sadistic, Himmler was actually squeamish about the details of mass murder and issued official instructions that SS officials were not to torment the inmates of the camps. In 1943 an SS officer was sentenced to death for succumbing to the temptation to 'commit atrocities unworthy of a German or an SS commander'.[20] Rudolf Hoess always maintained that he was doing to the best of his ability the job allocated to him and that, at the same time, he remained 'completely normal': 'Even while I was carrying out the task of extermination I led a normal family life. I never grew indifferent to human suffering.'[21]

By this route we arrive at a preposterous conclusion. Among the sadists handling the extermination programme were 'normal' family men, who presided over them and tried to do their duty like decent German citizens. The extermination programme was seen as an arduous duty to be carried out. It actually involved the denial of the preferences of the participant, not their sublimation. But this was the clue. Denial of preference was initially directed by external discipline. External discipline led to internal self-discipline as the participant adapted to a new routine. Routine brought familiarity with the task which, in turn, reduced the chance of rejecting it. Yet in all this, some absolute values could remain. These were parallel to and yet entirely cut off from the genocidal tasks being carried out. Hence men like Hoess, who remained a practising Catholic whilst Commandant at Auschwitz, literally led double lives, neither of which intruded on the other. We are left with the image of evil, in the words of Arendt, as being essentially 'banal'. In its ordinariness it can affect any group of people at any time. This is a far more frightening concept than a system dominated by psychopaths. Yet, for all that, evil can operate as banality only in the most extraordinary situations. This brings us full circle back to trying to understand the nature of the ideology and regime which managed to capture a cultured and civilised people.

Questions

1. Was the Holocaust 'deliberate'?
2. 'The Holocaust was a Nazi crime in which Germany shared.' Discuss.

ANALYSIS (3): HOW DID JEWS REACT TO PERSECUTION?

Most studies in racism and anti-semitism focus on the motivation of the persecutors. We also need to look at the reaction of the persecuted.

One view is that there was little resistance – and for a reason. According to Hilberg, the Jews tried to avoid provoking the Nazis into still more radical measures. 'They hoped that somehow the German drive would spend itself.' Furthermore 'This hope was founded on a two-thousand-year-old experience. In exile the Jews had always been a minority; they had always been in danger; but they had learned that they could avert danger and survive destruction by placating and appeasing their enemies.'[22] This may have been broadly true. Traditionally the Jews had survived by adapting to persecution rather than resisting it. Yet we should not conclude from this that there was no attempt to contest Nazi measures against them. This was actually done in a variety of ways.

There were, for example, numerous self-help organisations. Comprising lawyers, doctors and artists, these were intended to evade the discriminatory legislation where possible and to minimise its effects. These were also linked to the Reich Association of German Jews which tried periodic public appeals: in 1935, for example, it complained to the Minister of War about the exclusion of Jewish servicemen from the German armed forces. Jewish lawyers also complained to the League of Nations about discrimination in Upper Silesia, still officially under League supervision as a plebiscite area. In this instance the government backed down and withdrew some of its measures (although it reinstated them when the League's supervision ended in 1937). More radical opponents were prominent in the illegal groups organised by the Communists and Social Democrats. These, according to confidential Gestapo reports, contained a disproportionately large number of Jews. It is unlikely that such reports would have distorted this point, since they were intended to collate information not to press propaganda.

Yet in a sense such measures were counterproductive. Winterfelt argues that the various organisations impeded the full realisation of the extent of anti-semitism. The only real alternative was emigration, which the response actually discouraged. 'Instead of trying to make life for Jews under Nazi tyranny as pleasant as possible, everything, and every possible Pfennig, should have been invested in attempting to get Jews out of the country.'[23] There is some support for this: the United States allowed an annual immigration quota of 25,000, which was never filled before 1939.[24] On the other hand, different figures show that there was a major concerted effort to leave Germany. Of the Jewish population 130,000, or 20 per cent, emigrated between 1933 and 1937, while a further 118,000 followed them after Kristallnacht, leaving something like 164,000. This occurred despite the upheaval and dislocation, and the loss of up to 96 per cent of emigrants' financial assets. Housden therefore puts a different case to Winterfelt. 'If emigration amounted to opposition through escape, the vast majority of the Jews did oppose the Third Reich.'[25]

Perhaps not surprisingly, historical controversy intensifies over the period of the Holocaust between 1941 and 1945. One debate concerns the extent of the Jewish administrative co-operation with the authorities. As the Germans occupied eastern Europe they established Jewish authorities, or *Judenräte*, in areas of heavy Jewish population. In the ghetto of Lodz, for example, the *Judenräte* organised labour rotas, enforced discipline and prepared people for the resettlement ordered by the Nazis. Hilberg argues that the *Judenräte* aimed to avoid provoking the German authorities by making themselves indispensable to the German war economy. Actually, they did a great deal to help the German administration, the resources of which were heavily stretched. 'The Jewish and German policies, at first glance opposites, were in reality pointed in the same direction.'[26] In some cases Jewish officials even knew the secret of the exterminations – but decided to remain silent. While accepting the humanitarian motive behind this, some historians, like Robinson, see it nevertheless as 'collaboration'.[27] Against this, it is strongly arguable that without such co-operation the plight of the victims would have been even worse. The same applies to those *Judenräte* in Upper Silesia which tried to stamp out opposition to the Nazis and sometimes handed offenders over to the Gestapo. But, according to Trunk, 'Under the system of collective responsibility, any act of a single person could lead to collective punishment of the whole ghetto community, whose doom would then be sealed'.[28] What the *Judenräte* were doing, therefore, was to govern humanely. The fact that their authority was delegated to them by an inhumane system does not make them complicit.

Much has also been written about compliance within the death camps, especially over the apparent docility with which millions of Jews went to the gas chambers. One argument is the sheer extent of the deception applied by the Nazi authorities. Deportees were led to believe that they were being taken to the camps to be resettled. The next, and cruellest, deception was that those selected for the gas chambers were told that they were to be showered and deloused before taking on new trades allocated to them: they would therefore have been preparing themselves for a revival of the type of existence they had experienced in the ghettos. In these instances the SS and the German administration became expert at avoiding any trouble by building up hopes. Even in such terrible circumstances, however, there were examples of Jewish resistance. In 1942 Jewish inmates in Sachsenhausen rioted in protest against a decision to move them to the east. This was the only instance in Germany but there were also examples in 1943 at Treblinka, with 750 escapes, and at Sobibor with 300 breakouts. Meanwhile, in Berlin, the Herbert Baum Group in Berlin co-ordinated Jewish opposition, distributed anti-Nazi propaganda and made common cause with the Communists.

The way in which anti-semitism and the Holocaust were launched were paradoxical. On the one hand they seem to have been anticipated with open statements of intention. This would seem to indicate that the Jewish population had time to prepare some sort of reaction. On the other hand, the regime made this impossible by the nature of its measures. In the 1930s, deprivation of any legal status meant that any opposition was by definition illegal and consequently posed all types of moral dilemmas since it endangered the security of the whole community. The period of the Holocaust involved closer administrative co-operation and hence intensified this dilemma. This was partly a deliberate tactic by the Nazis to minimise resistance but also partly a means of reducing the administrative problems it faced – a combination perhaps of the intentionalist and functionalist approaches both to the Nazi regime and to its most evil perpetration.

Questions

1. Has the resistance of Jewish people to persecution and extermination been underestimated?
2. What predicaments would have faced the Jewish people in their response to Nazi authority between 1933 and 1945?

SOURCES

Source A: from an article written by Goebbels, 30 July 1928.

'Isn't the Jew a human being too?' Of course he is; none of us ever doubted it. All we doubt is that he is a decent human being.

Source B: from Hitler's speech to the Reichstag, 30 January 1939.

In the course of my life I have very often been a prophet, and have usually been ridiculed for it ... Today I will once more be a prophet: if the international Jewish financiers in and outside Europe should succeed in plunging the nations once more into a world war, then the result will not be the Bolshevizing of the earth, and thus the victory of Jewry, but the annihilation of the Jewish race in Europe!

Source C: from an article by Goebbels, 16 November 1941.

So, superfluous though it might be, let me say once more:
1. The Jews are our destruction. They provoked and brought about this war. What they mean to achieve by it is to destroy the German state and nation. This plan must be frustrated . . .
3. Every German soldier's death in this war is the Jews' responsibility. They have it on their conscience; hence they must pay for it . . .
9. A decent enemy, after his defeat, deserves our generosity. But the Jew is no decent enemy. He only pretends to be one.
10. The Jews are to be blamed for this war. The treatment we give them does them no wrong. They have more than deserved it.

Source D: from the diary of a Polish visitor to the Warsaw ghetto, Stanislav Rozycki, 1941.

The majority are nightmare figures, ghosts of former beings, miserable destitutes, pathetic remnants of former humanity . . .

On the streets children are crying in vain, children who are dying of hunger. They howl, beg, sing, moan, shiver with cold, without underwear, without clothing, without shoes, in rags, sacks, flannel which are bound in strips round the emaciated skeletons, children swollen with hunger, disfigured, half conscious, already completely grown up at the age of five, gloomy and weary of life. They are like old people and are only conscious of one thing: 'I'm cold.' I'm hungry . . . '

I no longer look at people; when I hear groaning and sobbing I go over to the other side of the road; when I see something wrapped in rags shivering with cold, stretched out on the ground, I turn away and do not want to look. I can't. It's become too much for me. And yet only an hour has passed.

Source E: from Himmler's speech to SS officers in Posen, 4 October 1943.

I also want to talk to you quite frankly about a very grave matter. We can talk about it quite frankly among ourselves and yet we will never speak of it publicly. Just as we did not hesitate on 30 June 1934 to do our duty as we were bidden, and to stand comrades who had lapsed up against the wall and shoot them, so we have never spoken about it and will never speak of it . . .

I am referring to the Jewish evacuation programme, the extermination of the Jewish people. It is one of those things which are easy to talk about. 'The

Jewish people will be exterminated' says every party comrade, 'It's clear, it's in our programme. Elimination of the Jews, extermination and we'll do it.' . . . To have stuck it out and – apart from a few exceptions due to human weakness – to have remained decent, that is what has made us tough. This is a glorious page in our history and one that has never been written and can never be written.

Source F: from evidence provided at a postwar trial of former SS guards at Sobibor.

The Jewish workers were at the complete mercy of the German camp guards who were the lords of the camp. Most of them had a very limited education, were completely under the influence of the major Nazi figures and their anti-semitic ideology and in most cases their moral sense had been totally blunted by their activity in the euthanasia centres. Their relations with the prisoners who – as they knew – were nothing but work slaves, who were living on borrowed time, but who were often far more highly educated than themselves, generated among a number of them a sense of superiority and primitive cravings for power and domination.

Source G: Rudolf Hoess giving evidence at his trial after the war.

I am completely normal. Even while I was carrying out the task of extermination I led a normal family life. I never grew indifferent to human suffering. I have always seen and felt for it . . . From our entire training the thought of refusing an order just didn't enter one's head, regardless of what kind of order it was.

Questions

1. What official positions were occupied by Goebbels (Sources A and C), Himmler (Source E) and Hoess? (Source G) [3]
2. Is Source B conclusive evidence that Hitler always intended an extermination programme? [5]
3. Comment on the content, language and tone of the description of the Warsaw ghetto in Source D. [6]
4. How much do Sources E, F and G show of the mentality of the SS officials? [5]
*5. 'In its anti-semitic policies the Nazi leadership destroyed all notions of "decency".' Comment on this in the light of these sources and your own knowledge. [6]

Worked answer

The wording of this question should not be seen as licence to express emotive viewpoints; despite the horrific nature of the subject the approach must remain firmly historical and rooted in the evidence.]

It is clear from Sources . . . that Nazi concepts of 'decency' were highly selective, compared with the more universal values prevalent in an open society. 'Decency' was taken automatically to exclude the Jews, as Goebbels stated in Source A. Indeed, Sources B and C point to the alleged danger posed by Jews to German society: 'The Jews are our destruction.' Hence, they could not be construed as 'a decent enemy' and, as such, were worthy of no normal consideration. The logic of this was that Germans could take radical measures against the Jews while, in the words of Himmler, ensuring that they 'remained decent' (Source E). This was taken even further by Hoess, who could claim to be 'completely normal' and even while 'carrying out the task of extermination' to have led 'a normal family life' (Source G). The reason for this capacity to lead two lives is hinted at in Source F: the 'influence of the major Nazi figures and their anti-semitic ideology'. This was in overall contrast to a civilian who had not been exposed to this and reacted in the more normal way shown in Source D: 'I turn away and do not want to look. I can't. It's become too much for me.'

There is plenty of additional evidence to support the existence of these double standards and the delusion that the persecutors were able to retain their decency. Acts of violent anti-semitism, such as Kristallnacht (1938) had been justified as 'righteous indignation' against Jewish exploitation, while the ethic of devotion to duty – even the unpleasant one of extermination – had already been rehearsed in the euthanasia programme for the mentally ill, referred to in Source F. It is also known that Himmler issued regulations for the punishment of SS officials who sullied this duty by acts of sadism. Such was the twist in logic that evil acts were sanitised and made to appear commonplace, as shown by Arendt's description of 'the banality of evil'.

7

FOREIGN POLICY AND WAR

BACKGROUND NARRATIVE

On coming to power in January 1933, Hitler had of necessity to pursue a cautious policy abroad while consolidating his position at home. His first move, however, was to remove Germany from the League of Nations Disarmament Conference. He argued that the proposals would have stripped Germany of the means of self-defence. He followed this by withdrawal from the League itself, an action heavily endorsed by a plebiscite within Germany. In 1934 Hitler sought to allay suspicion that he was preparing a general offensive by drawing up a Non-Aggression Pact with Poland.

Meanwhile, between 1933 and 1935, Hitler had begun to undermine the armaments limitation clauses of the Treaty of Versailles. By 1934 he had broken the limits imposed on the armed forces and in 1935 he announced the creation of an airforce and the introduction of conscription. Britain, France and Italy showed initial concern about these developments and came together in the Stresa Front. This, however, rapidly disintegrated. Italy became involved in a campaign in Abyssinia, in response to which Britain and France imposed sanctions on Italy. Britain also sought to draw up its own armaments settlement with Germany in the form of the Anglo-German Naval Agreement of 1935. Hitler used this apparent softening of the potential opposition against him to remilitarise the Rhineland in 1936, again in direct defiance of a key clause of the Treaty of Versailles. In the same year he provided German assistance to Franco and the Nationalist side in the Spanish Civil War, and drew up the Rome–Berlin Axis with Italy and the Anti-Comintern Pact with Japan. He also announced the Four Year Plan which was designed to accelerate rearmament and place the German economy on a war footing (see Chapter 5). In 1937 he stepped up the pace: the Hossbach Memorandum records a meeting between Hitler and his chiefs of staff in which Hitler stated that Germany must be prepared for war with the western powers, especially France, by 1942–3 at the latest. In 1938 he took advantage of the Anglo-French policy of appeasement by annexing Austria in the *Anschluss* and, in September by forcing Chamberlain, the British Prime Minister, to agree to the German annexation of the Sudetenland from Czechoslovakia. In March 1939 Hitler proceeded to occupy the rest of Bohemia, at which point Britain and France extended guarantees to Poland and Romania. Hitler proceeded, in August 1939, to form a Non-Aggression Pact with the Soviet Union. This contained a secret additional protocol to divide Poland between the two signatories. In his quest to enforce the territorial terms, Hitler invaded Poland on 1 September. This provoked Britain and France into declaring war on Germany on 2 and 3 September respectively.

The first stage of the war proved a spectacular success for Germany. Poland fell within weeks and the western half was absorbed into the Reich. In spring 1940 Hitler conquered Denmark, Norway, the Netherlands and Belgium, while France was defeated in June. All this was a spectacular success for the military strategy of *Blitzkrieg*. The subsequent attempt to prepare an invasion across the Channel was frustrated by the Battle of Britain. By June 1941 Hitler had lost interest in Operation Sealion and concentrated instead on Operation Barbarossa against Russia.

This opened up a new phase, generally referred to as one of 'total war'. Despite initial German victories, the Soviet Union recovered in 1942 and stemmed the German advance – especially at Stalingrad (1943). At the same time, the tide was also turning in North Africa, to which Hitler had been forced to send German troops to reverse the disastrous defeats suffered there by the Italians at the hands of the British. Total war assumed a global aspect when, in December 1941, Germany's ally, Japan, attacked Pearl Harbor. Hitler declared war on the United States in support of Japan, only to find that President Roosevelt made the decision to give priority to the war in Europe.

In 1944 Hitler was therefore confronted by the advancing Russians from the east and the Anglo-American forces from the south and west, while German cities were pounded by heavy bombing. Out-produced and outnumbered by the Allies, Germany surrendered, following Hitler's suicide on 30 April 1945.

ANALYSIS (1): HOW 'INTENTIONAL' WAS HITLER'S FOREIGN POLICY?

As in the domestic sphere, German foreign policy from 1933 has come within the scope of the broad debate between historians. Some, like Trevor-Roper, have argued that Hitler had plans which were 'unmistakably stated in *Mein Kampf* and that all the evidence of the 1930s shows that Hitler intended to carry them out'.[1] Indeed, *Mein Kampf* was 'a complete blueprint of his intended achievements'.[2]

To an extent this seems to be supported by evidence from *Mein Kampf*, which is quite explicit about 'The acquisition of land and soil as the objective of our foreign policy'. This should not settle for the 'restoration of the frontiers of 1914', which would be 'a political absurdity'. Instead, it meant expansion. But it is really the *Zweites Buch* which provides what might be described as a 'programme'. Written in 1928, this constructed a foreign policy programme of five stages. The first was the removal of the restrictions of Versailles, including the demilitarisation of the Rhineland. The second stage was the end of the French system of alliances in eastern Europe and the establishment of Germany's control over Austria, Czechoslovakia and Poland. The third would be the defeat of France. The fourth would then be the invasion of Russia, the fifth a contest for world supremacy possibly against Britain and the United States.[3] This source in particular has led more recent historians like Jäckel to believe that there is 'ample documentary evidence to prove that he always kept this programme in mind'.[4] Certainly there is a close parallel with what actually happened. The disarmament provisions of the Treaty of Versailles were reversed between 1934 and 1935 and the Rhineland remilitarised in 1936; Austria was taken over in 1938, as was the Sudetenland of Czechoslovakia, with Bohemia following in March 1939 and Poland in September; France was invaded in 1940; Operation Barbarossa was launched in 1941; and Hitler declared war on the United States in 1942. Since this seems to replicate the programme in the *Zweites Buch* with some precision, the case for premeditation must be a strong one.

This is not, however, the view of A. J. P. Taylor. In his *Origins of the Second World War*, Taylor argued that Hitler was above all an opportunist. 'Hitler did not make plans – for world conquest or for anything else. He assumed that others would provide opportunities and that he would seize them.'[5] His projects for expansion and conquest were 'in large part day-dreaming, unrelated to what followed in real life'. Hence 'Hitler was gambling on some twist of fortune which would present him with success in foreign affairs, just as a miracle had made him Chancellor in 1933.' The implication of this line of reasoning is that the sequence of events was entirely fortuitous and controlled by external factors rather than by Hitler himself. There may well be some evidence for this. Hitler was given his opportunity to remilitarise the Rhineland by the diversion of Britain and France against Italian aggression in Abyssinia the year before. He was able to take Austria with so little effort because Mussolini, who had originally opposed German schemes there, was now concentrating on an expanded overseas empire. The Sudetenland went Hitler's way because of the ardent desire of Chamberlain to avoid a European conflagration which the lessons of the Spanish Civil War seemed to suggest might happen all too easily. The outbreak of war in 1939 was not the deliberate upgrading of policy but rather Hitler's misreading of the Anglo-French guarantee made to Poland in March. The overall effect of Taylor's work was to place Hitler on a level with other statesmen in Europe, to emphasise that he, like they, was pragmatic. This made him appear less in control – and hence less demonic.

Taylor's thesis was a refreshingly different view but it has not stood the test of time. It is open to criticism on a variety of grounds. These all relate to the narrowness of its scope. Mason, for example, picks Taylor up for 'an overwhelming concentration on the sequence of diplomatic events'.[6] As such, it could be argued, the diplomatic focus ignores two important trends which contributed to Hitler's foreign policy. These may be seen as neither intentionalist nor pragmatic in the sense that Taylor meant. In other words, Taylor's revisionism has in turn been revised, without, however, a return to the original emphasis. Instead, there has been more emphasis on the operation of other forces and influences upon Hitler.

One of these was the past traditions of German foreign policy. German historians have established a considerable degree of continuity between the objectives of Hitler on the one hand and those of the Second Reich and the Weimar Republic on the other. Fischer, for one, maintains that Germany was on an expansionist path well before the Nazi era and that Hitler enlarged this into a concept of

Lebensraum.[7] There is much to support this. Germany's aims during the First World War were extensive. They comprised economic control over Belgium Holland and France in the west; domination of Poland and the Baltic coastline in the east, as well as over Serbia, Bulgaria and Romania in the Balkans; unification with Austria and the establishment of a Greater Germany; rule over a dismantled Russia; and hegemony over the eastern Mediterranean and Turkey. Hitler therefore had precedents in his aim to expand Germany's frontiers. It is true that he provided a more strongly *völkisch* and racialist slant to his foreign policy, but even here his views had been anticipated: Chapter 4 shows the origins of *Lebensraum* among pre-1914 fringe groups. If the Second Reich provided Hitler with at least some of his long-term objectives, the Weimar Republic helped shape his early approach. The policy of Stresemann, Foreign Minister between 1923 and 1929, had focused on the revision of the Treaty of Versailles, and the army, under von Seeckt, had already begun to evade the military restrictions imposed on Germany in 1919. Hitler continued and accelerated the process between 1933 and 1936 – until, by 1937, he was sufficiently confident to revive the more expansionist aims of the Second Reich.

A second influence on Hitler's foreign policy was the domestic economy. This is dealt with in more detail in Chapter 5. Recent historians have argued strongly that there is a direct correlation between Germany's economic problems and performance and the pursuit of an expansionist policy in Europe. Sauer maintains that *Blitzkrieg* was an economic as well as a military strategy. It was developed to enable Germany to increase rearmament without causing the German consumer excessive suffering and thereby depriving the regime of its support.[8] The practical effect was the deliberate dismantling of neighbouring states in order to strengthen the German economic base. Kershaw sees the relationship between the economy and militarism as more problematic. Hitler's Four Year Plan and his Hossbach Memorandum were a response to the economic crisis of 1935–6 and locked Germany into a course of rearmament – and war.[9] The process was less deliberate than Sauer maintains – but no less inexorable. It could also be argued that Hitler accelerated the pace of his foreign policy in order to divert German public opinion from domestic problems, especially economic. This was a well-worn device, used both in the Second Reich and in Mussolini's Italy.

What are we to make of these apparently contrasting views? There is a certain logic to all of them, but they need to be carefully integrated within an overall argument containing four main components. First, Hitler was not uniquely responsible for creating an entirely personal foreign policy. As Fischer has shown, he inherited the main hegemonist aims from the Second Reich. Nevertheless, second, he played an important part in renovating these within the context of a more forceful ideology based on a racial and *völkisch* vision, contained in *Mein Kampf* and the *Zweites Buch*. He therefore personalised and amended certain historical concepts, and it would be quite wrong to suggest that these were not seriously intended. Whether they amounted to a programme or a blueprint is, however, more questionable. Third, he implemented these ideas in his move towards war during the late 1930s partly as a result of the shaping of the German economy: the balance between guns and butter required a *Blitzkrieg* approach to conquest. Hence the Four Year Plan stepped up rearmament and the Hossbach Memorandum (1937) set an agenda for conflict. By 1938 internal forces had locked Germany into a course which was likely to lead to war. Only at this point can Taylor's thesis be included. With growing confidence provided by his military preparations, Hitler became more and more opportunist, playing the diplomatic system with some skill and achieving what he wanted over the *Anschluss* and the Sudetenland, before misinterpreting Chamberlain's stand in 1939 and falling into war at that point by accident.

Overall, Hitler was influenced by internal trends and pressures but, at the same time, he controlled the outlet points at which these pressures emerged. It was therefore Hitler who decided how internal trends should be translated into external action. This is, of course, far more than mere pragmatism, or opportunist reaction. But it is not quite as much as masterplanning or blueprinting. The debate has therefore moved on from Taylor and Trevor-Roper and is unlikely to return to them in the future.

Questions

1. What was 'new' about Hitler's foreign policy?
2. Should the Second World War be described as 'Hitler's war'?

ANALYSIS (2): DID HITLER CONTROL THE DEVELOPMENT OF THE SECOND WORLD WAR?

The controversy about the development of Hitler's foreign policy up to the outbreak of war in 1939 has its parallel in his involvement in the war itself. Did he control its various stages, converting initial victory to eventual defeat through the defects of his obsessive personal leadership? Or were his decisions largely shaped by factors beyond his control? The answer to these questions depends very much on the type of war actually fought. By and large, it could be argued that Hitler dominated the phase generally described as *Blitzkrieg*, while the total war which followed he found increasingly problematic.

There is considerable evidence that Hitler dominated the *Blitzkrieg* phase. This involved the core areas of Europe and saw a deliberate expansion of Germany's frontiers at the expense of weaker opponents like Poland. This fitted well with the economic objectives of the Nazi regime, which were to achieve conquest without too high a cost to the German consumer. The Non-Aggression Pact with the Soviet Union (August 1939) was intended to facilitate the process and to avoid any possibility of a long and drawn-out war at this stage. Once Poland had been destroyed, Hitler also set the agenda for the conflict in western Europe. Britain and France had taken no direct military action between September 1938 and the spring of 1939 and it was on Hitler's initiative that the war spread to Denmark, Norway, the Netherlands, Belgium and France. In the case of France, the initiative seems to have been entirely a personal one, since the German High Command warned against the invasion in June 1940. The result was, however, a spectacular victory for the German *Panzer* divisions who bypassed the Maginot Line and the French defences on the Belgian frontier with a rapid advance through the Ardennes.

To an extent, therefore, we can refer to the early stage of the conflict as 'Hitler's war'. It seems to accord with long-term objectives to achieve *Lebensraum*, to defeat the country most likely to prevent this – France – and to implement the timetable implicit in the Hossbach Memorandum. Yet even at this early stage Hitler was confronted by two factors beyond his immediate control. One was his inability to detach Britain from the conflict by means of a negotiated settlement, followed by the failure of the military solution – Operation Sealion. The Battle of Britain (1940) ensured that Germany would have to face the continued involvement of an undefeated power in the west. The second un-predictable occurrence in 1940 was the defeat of Italian troops in the Balkans by the Greeks and in North Africa by the British. Already the impact of *Blitzkrieg* was being undermined as Hitler was having to spread his forces more thinly away from the core of Europe into the periphery. This was the type of warfare which suited Britain, not Germany.

When Hitler launched Operation Barbarossa on the Soviet Union in June 1941, it seemed that he had recaptured the initiative. But was this his own decision? It is possible to present this in two very different interpretations.

On the one hand, it is normally argued that the attack on the Soviet Union was the culmination of everything he had ever believed. In *Mein Kampf* he had maintained that Germany must focus on the east: 'we must principally bear in mind Russia and the border states subject to her'. Russia had become an alien state now that it had been taken over by 'the Jewish yoke'. Jäckel, too, maintains that 'Hitler's main aim in foreign policy was a war of conquest against the Soviet Union.'[10] By this analysis, therefore, the spread of the war into the plains of eastern Europe was a decision – ultimately to prove disastrous – taken by Hitler. It was against the advice of his High Command and in defiance of the logic of not opening up a second front before the first had been properly closed down. But it was deliberate.

An alternative argument could be put forward, although more speculatively. It might be possible to see Hitler's decision to launch Operation Barbarossa in June 1941 as a pre-emptive strike. He perceived the Soviet Union less as a race and ideological enemy than as a looming military threat which would become more and more serious unless it was dealt with immediately. Stalin's military expenditure throughout the 1930s had been as high as Hitler's and the Soviet workforce was being prepared for total war in a way which the German workforce was not. By June 1941 the Red Army stood at 5.4 million. It also had more tanks than all the other countries of the world together.[11] Aircraft production far outran that of Germany and new industrial complexes were springing up in the east, out of the range of German bombers. It must have seemed to Hitler that the gap was growing rapidly between the military strengths of the two powers. Bearing in mind the strategy announced in the Hossbach Memorandum to deal with the west sooner rather than later, might the same not apply to the Soviet Union? After all, Hitler's hands were free: France had been smashed and Britain, although undefeated, was unable to bring the war to the continent. The most appropriate time for another strike was 1941, particularly since the Red Army had recently lost many of its most able officers as a result of Stalin's purges. Indeed, it is possible that Stalin was preparing action of his own against Germany for the near or intermediate future. Although there is little direct evidence of this at the moment, this would hardly have been released by the Soviet government after the war. The opening up of the archives in post-Soviet Russia could well reveal a very different perspective and provide support for the theory that Hitler considered that he was forced by Stalin into making a preventive strike.

A similar dichotomy exists over the declaration of war on the United States. According to Hillgruber, Hitler's policy was 'designed to span the globe; ideologically, too, the doctrines of universal anti-semitism and social Darwinism, fundamental to his programme, were intended to embrace the whole of mankind'.[12] Hildebrand and Hauner also see this stage as the pursuit of global domination. On the other hand, where was the sense of voluntarily extending the conflict from the continent to the periphery? Germany was already hard pressed in North Africa and would be further weakened by maritime involvements. In any case, Hitler had once claimed in his *Zweites Buch* that the major mistake of the Second Reich was to challenge for imperial and maritime supremacy before imposing control over the continent. The answer must, therefore, be that circumstances pushed Hitler into a course of action which he would have preferred to avoid. The Japanese attack on Pearl Harbor involved the United States in a conflict which was bound to link up in an alliance with Britain. Hitler was therefore bolstering up Japan in the belief that the United States would be kept preoccupied by the Japanese in the Pacific until Germany had won the war in Europe. Roosevelt's decision to give priority to the defeat of Germany shows that Hitler's logic was flawed – but also that this made very little difference to the outcome. Hitler had very little control over the arrival of war between Germany and the United States.

It seems therefore that, although he did have long-term objectives, Hitler tended to defer them when the time was unfavourable and to adopt them when obliged by circumstances to do so. This means that he was less in control of the situation than is often thought. This brings a structuralist emphasis even to what is generally seen as the biggest personal decision – and error – of Hitler's entire career. Hence he hated the Soviet Union and hoped eventually to destroy it. But the decision was taken under pressure. He also considered it likely that Germany would have to contest global supremacy with the United States, but he declared war only after the USA was brought in as a result of the Japanese connection.

How could Hitler have countenanced such a spread in the conflict, given the enormous disparity of resources between Germany and the Anglo-Soviet-American combination? Again, there are two possibilities. One is that Hitler had become blind to all military reason and oblivious to advice. The popular perception of Hitler is that he succumbed to megalomania from 1941 onwards and personally dragged Germany to defeat and destruction in the mistaken belief that he could bring ultimate and total victory. This would be an argument based on Intentionalism gone wrong: he created his own pressures. The alternative is that Hitler was under external pressures and that he tried to respond to them in ways that had worked before. Hence the solution was to use

Blitzkrieg against larger opponents. It failed because it was never intended for use in this way.

Questions

1. 'Hitler lost control over the course of the war. That is why he lost the war.' Discuss.
2. What questions remained to be answered about the way in which '*Blitzkrieg*' developed into 'total war'?

SOURCES

1. PEACE OR WAR?

Source A: from the Hossbach Memorandum, a record made by Colonel Hossbach of a confidential meeting between Hitler and the chiefs of German staff, 5 November 1937.

The Führer then continued:

The aim of German policy was to make secure and to preserve the racial community and to enlarge it. It was therefore a question of space.

The German community comprised over 85 million people and, by reason of their number and the narrow limits of habitable space in Europe, it constituted a tightly packed racial core such as was not to be found in any other country and such as implied the right to a greater living space than in the case of other peoples. If there existed no political result, territorially speaking, corresponding to this German racial core, that was a consequence of centuries of historical development, and in the continuance of these political conditions lay the greatest danger to the preservation of the German race at its present peak.

Source B: extracts from a reported conversation between Hitler and Lord Halifax on 19 November 1937.

Hitler: There were two possibilities in the shaping of relations between the peoples: the interplay of free forces, which was often synonymous with great and grave encroachments upon the life of the peoples and which could bring in its train a serious convulsion which would shake the civilisation we had built up with so much trouble. The second possibility lay in setting up in place of the play of free forces the rule of 'higher reason' ... In the year 1919 a great chance to apply this method had been missed. At that time a solution of unreasonableness had been preferred: as a consequence Germany had been forced back on the path of the free play of forces, because this was the only possible way to make sure of the simplest rights of mankind. It would be decisive for the future whether the one method were chosen, or the other . . .

Halifax: On the English side, it was not necessarily thought that the status quo must be maintained under all circumstances . . . It was recognised that one might have to contemplate an adjustment to new conditions, a correction of former mistakes and the recognition of changed circumstances when such need arose. In doing so England made her influence felt only in one way – to secure that these alterations should not be made in a manner corresponding to the unreasonable solution mentioned by the Chancellor, the play of free forces, which in the end meant war. He must emphasise once more in the name of H.M. Government that possibility of change of the existing situation was not excluded, but that changes should only take place upon the basis of reasonable agreements reasonably reached.

Source C: from a secret speech made by Hitler to representatives of the German press at Munich, 10 November 1938.

We have set ourselves several tasks this year which we want to achieve through our propaganda – and I consider the press present here among the main instruments of our propaganda.

First, the gradual preparation of the people themselves. For years circumstances have compelled me to talk about almost nothing but peace. Only by continually stressing Germany's desire for peace and her peaceful intentions could I achieve freedom for the German people bit by bit and provide the armaments which were always necessary before the next step could be taken. It is obvious that such peace propaganda also has its doubtful aspects, for it can only too easily give people the idea that the present regime really identifies itself with the determination to preserve peace at all costs. That would not only lead to a wrong assessment of the aims of this system, but above all it might lead to the German nation, instead of being prepared for every eventuality, being filled with a spirit of defeatism which in the long run would inevitably undermine the success of the present regime. It is only out of necessity that for years I talked of peace. But it is now necessary gradually to re-educate the German people psychologically and to make it clear that there are things which must be achieved by force if peaceful means fail. To do this, it was necessary not to advocate force as such, but to depict to the German people certain diplomatic events in such a light that the inner voice of the nation itself gradually began to call for the use of force.

Questions

*1. (i) What German word is normally used for 'living space' in Source A? [1]

(ii) Explain the reference 'At that time a solution of unreasonableness had been preferred' (Source B). [2]

2. What are the main differences between the arguments and language used by Hitler in Sources A and B? How would you explain these differences? [6]

3. What does Source B show about the attitude of the British government towards Hitler's foreign policy objectives? [4]

4. What light does Source C throw on the arguments used by Hitler in Sources A and B? [4]

5. 'Hitler's foreign policy was geared to the inevitability of war.' Discuss this view in the light of Sources A to C and your own knowledge. [8]

Worked answer

*1. (i) *Lebensraum.*

(ii) The reference is to the Treaty of Versailles (1919). Hitler was echoing the popular view that the terms had been deliberately harsh on Germany.

SOURCES

2. WHAT TYPE OF WAR?

Source D: from Hitler's memorandum of 9 October 1939, to the commanders-in-chief of the army and navy, arguing for a rapid offensive against the west.

The first threat to Germany lies in the fact that if the war lasts a long time, in certain circumstances other States may be drawn into the opposing front either on grounds of economic necessity or through the development of particular interests.

The second danger lies in the fact that through a long drawn-out war States which might be basically favourable to joining Germany, in view of the experience of the last war, may take the very length of the war as a warning and therefore avoid intervening on our behalf.

The third danger involved in a lengthy war lies in the difficulty of feeding our population and securing the means of fighting the war in view of the limited basis for food supplies and raw materials. The morale of the population will at the very least be adversely affected.

Source E: from Hitler's military directive for the invasion of Russia.

The German *Wehrmacht* must be prepared to crush Soviet Russia in a quick campaign (Operation Barbarossa) even before the conclusion of the war against England.

For this purpose the army will have to employ all available units . . .

For the Luftwaffe it will be a matter of releasing such strong forces for the eastern campaign in support of the army that a quick completion of the ground operation can be counted on . . .

The main effort of the navy will remain unequivocally directed against England, even during the eastern campaign . . .

The mass of the Russian army in western Russia is to be destroyed in daring operations, by driving forward deep armoured wedges; and the retreat of units capable of combat into the vastness of Russian territory is to be prevented . . .

In the course of these operations the Russian Baltic Sea Fleet will quickly lose its bases and thus will no longer be able to fight.

Effective intervention by the Russian Air Force is to be prevented by powerful blows at the very beginning of the operation.

Source F: from a record of a meeting between Hitler and the Japanese ambassador, Oshima, on 3 January 1942.

All of us and Japan as well were engaged in a joint life and death struggle and so it was vital that we share our military experience.

. . . Hitler then emphasized that it was probably the first time in history that two such powerful military powers, which were so far apart from one another, stood together in battle. Provided their military operations were coordinated, this offered the possibility of creating leverage in the conduct of the war which must have enormous effects on the enemy, since they would be thereby compelled continually to shift their centres of gravity and in this way would hopelessly fritter away their forces.

. . . The Führer is of the opinion that England can be destroyed. He is not yet sure how the USA can be defeated . . . England was the main enemy. We would certainly not be defeated by Russia.

Source G: from the Diary of the Italian Foreign Minister, Ciano, recording Hitler's meeting with Mussolini on 29 April 1942.

America is a big bluff. This slogan is repeated by everyone, big and little, in the conference rooms and in the antechambers. In my opinion, the thought of what the Americans can and will do disturbs them all, and the Germans shut their eyes to it. But this does not keep the more intelligent and the more honest from thinking about what America can do, and they feel shivers running down their spines.

Hitler talks, talks, talks, talks, talks. Mussolini suffers – he, who is in the habit of talking himself, and who, instead, has to remain practically silent.

Source H: from an account of Hitler's discussion with Mussolini, 22 April 1944.

The Führer would never under any circumstances capitulate . . .

The Führer had spent a lot of time reading history recently and had noted that most coalitions hardly lasted for five years. The fact that our allies had remained loyal to us, despite the long period of war, was only because Fascism ruled in Italy . . . Our enemies' coalition was unnatural. It involved two different worlds . . . In addition there was the conflict between England and America. America was quietly and without making a fuss about it plundering England . . . If one read the English and American press, one could see that tension was growing . . .

The most important thing was to hold on stubbornly at all events, since the front of our opponents must break down one day.

Questions

1. (i) Which country was Hitler referring to in his words 'States which might be basically favourable to joining Germany' (Source D)? [1]
   (ii) Which German term best describes the type of war Hitler proposed to use to avoid the predicament shown in Source D? What is the literal translation of this term? [2]
2. To what extent are the basic principles of Source D applied to the detailed directives in Source E? [4]
3. Comment on the reliability and usefulness of Source G as a record of Hitler's attitude towards the management of the war. [5]
4. Compare the argument used by Hitler in Source F with that in Source H. How would you explain the difference in emphasis? [5]
5. 'Hitler showed a consistent misunderstanding of Germany's capacity to wage successful war.' Comment on this view in the light of Sources D to H and your own knowledge. [8]

NOTES AND SOURCES

1. THE RISE OF NAZISM

1. Extracts from the Party Programme of 1920.
2. Quoted from *Mein Kampf* in G. Layton: *Germany: the Third Reich 1933–45* (London 1992), p. 20.
3. M. Broszat: *Hitler and the Collapse of the Weimar Republic* (Oxford 1987), p. 37.
4. M. Broszat: *Hitler and the Collapse of the Weimar Republic*, p. 37.
5. H. Trevor-Roper: *The Last Days of Hitler* (London 1968), p. 54.
6. See A. Bullock: *Hitler: A Study in Tyranny* (London: 1961).
7. Quoted in K. Hildebrand: *The Third Reich* (London 1984), p. 123.
8. This is covered in S. J. Lee: *The Weimar Republic*, in this series.
9. T. Childers: 'The middle classes and National Socialism', in D. Blackburn and R. J. Evans (eds): *The German Bourgeoisie* (London 1991), p. 326.
10. See T. Childers and J. Caplan (eds): *Reevaluating the Third Reich* (New York 1993).
11. P. D. Stachura: 'Who were the Nazis? A socio-political analysis of the National Socialist *Machtübernahme*', *European Studies Review*, 2, 1981.
12. D. Mulberger: 'The sociology of the NSDAP: The question of working class membership', *Journal of Contemporary History*, 15, 1980.
13. C. Fischer: *The Rise of the Nazis* (Manchester 1995), p. 108.
14. J. Hiden: *Republican and Fascist Germany* (London 1996), p. 60.
Source A: J. Remak (ed.): *The Nazi Years* (Englewood Cliffs, NJ 1969), pp. 28–9.
Source B: J. Remak (ed.): *The Nazi Years*, p. 32.
Source C: Hitler: *Mein Kampf* (1924).
Source D: Otto Strasser: *Hitler and I* (London 1940).

Source E: C. Fischer: *The Rise of the Nazis* (Manchester 1995), pp. 138–9.
Source F: Otto Strasser: *Hitler and I* (London 1940), p. 114.
Source H: adapted from C. Fischer: *The Rise of the Nazis* (Manchester 1995), p. 170.
Source I: adapted from C. Fischer: *The Rise of the Nazis*, p. 171.
Source J: C. Fischer: *The Rise of the Nazis*, p. 180.
Source K: C. Fischer: *The Rise of the Nazis*, pp. 179–80.

2. THE ESTABLISHMENT OF DICTATORSHIP

1. J. Remak (ed.): *The Nazi Years* (Englewood Cliffs, NJ 1969), p. 52.
2. See K. Hildebrand: *The Third Reich* (trans. London 1984), especially Concluding Remarks.
3. J. Noakes and G. Pridham: *Nazism 1919–1945: A Documentary Reader* (Exeter 1983–8), p. 256.
4. K. D. Bracher: *The German Dictatorship* (New York 1970).
5. K. Hildebrand: *The Third Reich*.
6. M. Broszat: *Hitler and the Collapse of the Weimar Republic* (Oxford 1987).
7. See also extracts from H. Mommsen in K. Hildebrand: *The Third Reich*, p. 137.
Source A: L. L. Snyder: *The Weimar Republic* (Princeton, NJ 1966), Reading no. 18.
Source B: J. Remak (ed.): *The Nazi Years*, pp. 52–3.
Source C: J. Remak (ed.): *The Nazi Years*, p. 54.
Source D: J. Noakes and G. Pridham: *Nazism*, p. 185.
Source E: J. Laver: *Nazi Germany 1933–1945* (London 1991), p. 12.
Source G: J. Noakes and G. Pridham: *Nazism*, p. 252.
Source H: J. Noakes and G. Pridham: *Nazism*, p. 252.
Source I: J. Noakes and G. Pridham: *Nazism*, p. 207.
Source J: J. Noakes and G. Pridham: *Nazism*, p. 243.
Source K: J. Laver: *Nazi Germany*, p. 16.

3. INDOCTRINATION, PROPAGANDA AND TERROR

1. J. Noakes and G. Pridham: *Nazism 1919–1945: A Documentary Reader* (Exeter 1983–8), p. 381.
2. J. Hiden and J. Farquharson: *Explaining Hitler's Germany* (London 1983), p. 55.
3. D. J. K. Peukert: *Inside Nazi Germany* (trans. London 1987), p. 15.
4. J. Noakes and G. Pridham: *Nazism*, p. 493.

5. J. Noakes and G. Pridham: *Nazism*, p. 497.
6. H. Höhne: *The Order of the Death's Head* (London 1967), p. 12.
7. Quoted in K. M. Mallman and G. Paul: 'Omniscient, omnipotent, omnipresent? Gestapo, society and resistance', in D. F. Crew (ed.): *Nazism and German Society 1933–1945* (London 1994), p. 169.
8. K. M. Mallman and G. Paul: 'Omniscient', p. 169.
9. K. M. Mallman and G. Paul: 'Omniscient', pp. 169–70.
10. *Völkischer Beobachter*, 17 February 1941.
11. K. M. Mallman and G. Paul: 'Omniscient', p. 174.
12. J. Hiden: *Republican and Fascist Germany* (Harlow 1996), p. 181.
Source A: J. Noakes and G. Pridham *Nazism*, p. 334.
Source B: J. Noakes and G. Pridham *Nazism*, p. 382.
Source C: J. Noakes and G. Pridham *Nazism*, p. 386.
Source D: J. Noakes and G. Pridham *Nazism*, p. 394.
Source E: Louis P. Lochner, ed.: *The Goebbels Diaries, 1942–3* (Washington DC 1948) pp. 177–80.
Source F: T. Jones: *Lloyd George* (Cambridge, Mass 1951).
Source G: D. Orlow: *The History of the Nazi Party, vol. 2* (Newton Abbot 1971).
Source H: J. Noakes and G. Pridham: *Nazism*, p. 500.
Source I: J. Noakes and G. Pridham: *Nazism*, 495–6.
Source J: J. Noakes and G. Pridham: *Nazism*, p. 500.
Source K: J. Noakes and G. Pridham: *Nazism*, p. 514.
Source L: J. Laver: *Nazi Germany 1933–1945* (London 1991), pp. 73–4.

4. SUPPORT AND OPPOSITION

1. This was the view of a report by the Social Democratic Party in Exile (SOPADE); quoted in D. J. K. Peukert: *Inside Nazi Germany* (trans. London 1987), p. 71.
2. Quoted in D. J. Peukert: *Inside Nazi Germany*, p. 69.
3. Quoted in D. F. Crew: *Nazism and German Society, 1933–1945* (London 1994) pp. 4–5.
4. D. F. Crew: *Nazism and German Society*, p. 6.
5. D. J. K. Peukert: *Inside Nazi Germany*, p. 69.
6. R. Grunberger: *A Social History of the Third Reich* (London 1971).
7. Sir J. Wheeler-Bennett: *The Nemesis of Power: The German Army in Politics 1918–1945* (London 1953), part III, ch. 2.
8. O. Bartov: 'The missing years: German workers, German soldiers', in D. F. Crew (ed.): *Nazism and German Society 1933–1945*, p. 46.

9. See K. Mallmann and G. Paul: 'Omniscient, omnipotent, omni-present? Gestapo, society and resistance' in D. F. Crew (ed.): *Nazism and German Society*, pp. 180–9.
10. See D. J. Goldhagen: *Hitler's Willing Executioners: Ordinary Germans and the Holocaust* (London 1997), especially ch. 15.
11. I. Kershaw: *Popular Opinion and Political Dissent in the Third Reich* (Oxford 1983), p. 373.
12. Quoted in I. Kershaw: *Popular Opinion*, p. 126.
13. D. Peukert: 'Youth in the Third Reich', in R. Bessel (ed.): *Life in the Third Reich* (Oxford 1987).
14. D. J. K. Peukert: *Inside Nazi Germany*, p. 248.
Source A: Hitler: *Mein Kampf*.
Source B: J. Dülffer: *Nazi Germany 1933–1945: Faith and Annihilation* (trans. London 1996), p. 90.
Source C: D. J. K. Peukert: *Inside Nazi Germany*, p. 74.
Source D: D. J. K. Peukert: *Inside Nazi Germany*, p. 195.
Source E: D. J. K. Peukert: *Inside Nazi Germany*, p. 109.
Source F: M. Housden: *Resistance and Conformity in the Third Reich* (London 1997) p. 51.
Source G: M. Housden: *Resistance and Conformity in the Third Reich*, p. 52.
Source H: M. Housden: *Resistance and Conformity in the Third Reich*, p. 52.
Source L: M. Housden: *Resistance and Conformity in the Third Reich*, p. 61.

5. THE NAZI ECONOMY

1. Hitler: *Mein Kampf* (1925), quoted in J. Laver (ed.): *Nazi Germany* (London 1991), p. 82.
2. Quoted in J. Remak (ed.) *The Nazi Years* (Englewood Cliffs, NJ 1969), pp. 32–3.
3. Extract in R. G. L. Waite (ed.): *Hitler and Nazi Germany* (New York 1965).
4. Extract in R. G. L. Waite (ed.): *Hitler and Nazi Germany*.
5. J. Hiden and J. Farquharson: *Explaining Hitler's Germany* (London 1983), p. 151.
6. V. R. Berghahn: *Modern Germany: Society, Economy and Politics in the Twentieth Century* (Cambridge 1987), p. 149.
7. Quoted in J. Noakes and G. Pridham: *Nazism 1919–1945: A Documentary Reader*, p. 684.
8. Quoted in G. Layton: *Germany: the Third Reich 1933–45* (London 1992), p. 77.
9. Quoted in G. Layton: *Germany: the Third Reich*, p. 77.

10. C. W. Guillebaud: *The Economic Recovery of Germany from 1933 to the Incorporation of Austria in March 1938* (London 1939).
11. V. R. Berghahn: *Modern Germany*, p. 284, table 18.
12. V. R. Berghahn: *Modern Germany* p. 290, table 25.
13. V. R. Berghahn: *Modern Germany*, p. 279, table 10.
Source A: V. R. Berghahn: *Modern Germany*, p. 284.
Source B: V. R. Berghahn: *Modern Germany*, p. 279.
Source G: J. Noakes and G. Pridham: *Nazism*, p. 298.
Source H: J. Noakes and G. Pridham: *Nazism*, pp. 281–7.
Source J: K. Hildebrand: *The Third Reich* (London 1984), p. 43.
Source K: J. Noakes and G. Pridham: *Nazism*, pp. 292–3.
Source L: J. Noakes and G. Pridham: *Nazism*, p. 292.

6. RACE, THE HOLOCAUST AND THE JEWISH RESPONSE

1. J. Remak (ed.): *The Nazi Years* (Englewood Cliffs, NJ 1969), p. 4.
2. Hitler: *Mein Kampf* (1925).
3. Hitler: *Mein Kampf*.
4. Hitler: *Zweites Buch* (1928).
5. D. J. K. Peukert: *Inside Nazi Germany* (trans. London 1987), p. 208. See also T. W. Mason: *Social Policy in the Third Reich: The Working Class and the 'National Community'* (Oxford 1993), pp. 279–80.
6. D. J. K. Peukert: *Inside Nazi Germany*, p. 209.
7. D. J. K. Peukert: *Inside Nazi Germany*, p. 233.
8. D. Schoenbaum: *Hitler's Social Revolution* (New York 1980), p. 55.
9. J. Remak (ed.): *The Nazi Years*, p. 5.
10. Hitler: *Mein Kampf*.
11. Streicher: *Der Stürmer*.
12. D. J. Goldhagen: *Hitler's Willing Executioners: Ordinary Germans and the Holocaust* (London 1996), p. 162.
13. See R. Hilberg: *The Destruction of the European Jews* (Chicago 1961).
14. See M. Kitchen: *Nazi Germany at War* (London 1995), p. 200.
15. J. Remak (ed.): *The Nazi Years*, p. 159.
16. J. Dülffer: *Nazi Germany 1933–1945: Faith and Annihilation* (trans. London 1996), p. 179.
17. D. J. Goldhagen: *Hitler's Willing Executioners*, p. 162.
18. Quoted in R. Breitman: 'The "Final Solution"', in G. Martel: *Modern Germany Reconsidered* (London 1992), p. 197.
19. Quoted in H. Höhne: *The Order of the Death's Head* (trans. London 1967), p. 352.

20. Quoted in H. Höhne: *The Order of the Death's Head*, p. 353.
21. J. Noakes and G. Pridham: *Nazism 1919–1945: A Documentary Reader* (Exeter 1984).
22. R. Hilberg: *The Destruction of the European Jews*, pp. 666–7.
23. Quoted in A. Barkai: *From Boycott to Annihilation* (London 1989), p. 141.
24. C. Koonz: *Mothers in the Fatherland. Women, the Family and Nazi Politics* (New York 1987), p. 363.
25. M. Housden: *Resistance and Conformity in the Third Reich* (London 1997), p. 125.
26. R. Hilberg: 'The Judenrät: conscious or unconscious tool?', in Y. Vashem: *Patterns of Jewish Leadership in Nazi Europe 1933–45: Proceedings of the Yad Vashem International Conference, Jerusalem, 1977.*
27. J. Robinson: 'Some basic issues that faced the Jewish councils', in I. Trunk: *Judenrät: The Jewish Councils in Eastern Europe under Nazi Occupation* (London 1972), p. xxxi.
28. I. Trunk: 'The attitude of the Judenrats to the problems of armed resistance against the Nazis', in Y. Vashem: *Patterns of Jewish Leadership*, p. 205.
Source A: J. Remak (ed.): *The Nazi Years*, p. 145.
Source B: J. Noakes and G. Pridham: *Nazism*, p. 1049.
Source C: J. Remak (ed.): *The Nazi Years*, p. 156.
Source D: J. Noakes and G. Pridham: *Nazism*, pp. 1067–8.
Source E: J. Noakes and G. Pridham: *Nazism*, p. 1199.
Source F: J. Noakes and G. Pridham: *Nazism*, p. 1204.

7. FOREIGN POLICY AND WAR

1. A. J. P. Taylor: 'Hitler and the War', *Encounter*, 17, July 1961.
2. Quoted in D. G. Williamson: *The Third Reich* (Harlow 1982), ch. 3.
3. J. Noakes and G. Pridham: *Nazism 1919–1945: A Documentary Reader*, pp. 617–18.
4. E. Jackel: *Hitler in History* (Hanover and London 1984), ch. 2.
5. A. J. P. Taylor: *The Origins of the Second World War* (London 1963), p. 172.
6. T. W. Mason: 'Some origins of the Second World War', *Past and Present*, 1964.
7. See F. Fischer: *Germany's Aims in the First World War* (London 1967).
8. See extract in R. G. L. Waite (ed.): *Hitler and Nazi Germany* (New York 1965).
9. I. Kershaw: lecture at Aston University; 1997.

10. E. Jackel: *Hitler in History*, ch. 2.
11. B. Bonwetsch: 'Stalin, the Red Army, and the "Great Patriotic War"', in I. Kershaw and M. Lewin (eds): *Stalinism and Nazism: Dictatorships in Comparison* (Cambridge 1997), p. 186.
12. A. Hillgruber: 'England's place in Hitler's plans for world dominion', *Journal of Contemporary History*, 9, 1974.

Source A: Documents on German Foreign Policy, Series D, vol. I, pp. 29ff.

Source B: Documents on German Foreign Policy, Series D, vol. I, pp. 55ff.

Source C: J. Noakes and G. Pridham: *Nazism*, pp. 721–2.

Source D: J. Noakes and G. Pridham: *Nazism*, p. 761.

Source E: Documents on German Foreign Policy, Series D, vol. XI, p. 52.

Source F: J. Noakes and G. Pridham: *Nazism*, pp. 836–7.

Source G: J. Noakes and G. Pridham: *Nazism*, p. 838.

Source H: J. Noakes and G. Pridham: *Nazism*, pp. 867–8.

SELECT BIBLIOGRAPHY

A vast number of books has been published on Nazi Germany. This list is therefore particularly selective.

The main primary sources are Hitler: *Mein Kampf* (1925) and Hitler: *Second Book* (1928). Selections of sources are to be found in J. Remak (ed.): *The Nazi Years* (Englewood Cliffs, NJ, 1969) and in the three volumes of J. Noakes and G. Pridham: *Nazism* (Exeter 1983–8).

Good introductions to the topic are G. Layton: *Germany and the Third Reich 1933–45* (London 1992) and D. G. Williamson: *The Third Reich* (Harlow 1982). Traditional texts, although now dated, are H. Trevor-Roper: *The Last Days of Hitler* (London 1968) and A. Bullock: *Hitler, A Study in Tyranny* (London 1961). More recent and vitally important German interpretations are M. Broszat: *Hitler and the Collapse of the Weimar Republic* (Oxford 1987), M. Broszat: *The Hitler State* (trans. London 1981), K. D. Bracher: *The German Dictatorship* (trans. London 1970), and K. Hildebrand: *The Third Reich* (London 1984).

Internal developments are covered in R. Grunberger: *A Social History of the Third Reich* (London 1971), D. J. K. Peukert: *Inside Nazi Germany* (trans. London 1987), D. Crew, (ed.): *Nazism and German Society 1933–1945* (London 1994), T. W. Mason: *Social Policy in the Third Reich: The Working Class and the 'National Community'* (Oxford 1993), D. Schaunbaum: *Hitler's Social Revolution* (New York 1980), I. Kershaw: *Popular Opinion and Political Dissent in the Third Reich* (Oxford 1983), J. Dülffer: *Nazi Germany 1933–1945: Faith and Annihilation* (trans. London 1996) and D. Blackburn and R. J. Evans (eds): *The German Bourgeoisie* (London 1991).

Excellent introductions or collections of essays are included in V. R. Berghahn: *Modern Germany: Society, Economy and Politics in the Twentieth Century* (Cambridge 1987), Martel: *Modern Germany Reconsidered* (London 1992), J. Hiden: *Republican and Fascist Germany* (London 1996), T. Childers and J. Caplan (eds): *Reevaluating the Third Reich* (New York 1993), and J. Hiden and J. Farquharson: *Explaining Hitler's Germany* (London 1983).

Foreign policy and Germany at war are covered in A. J. P. Taylor: *The Origins of the Second World War* (London 1963) and M. Kitchen: *Nazi Germany at War* (London 1995), with an excellent comparison with the Soviet Union available in I. Kershaw and M. Lewin (eds): *Stalinism and Nazism: Dictatorships in Comparison* (Cambridge 1997). The persecution of the Jews and the Holocaust are covered in D. J. Goldhagen: *Hitler's Willing Executioners: Ordinary Germans and the Holocaust* (London 1997), R. Hilberg: *The Destruction of the European Jews* (Chicago 1961) and A. Barkai: *From Boycott to Annihilation* (London 1989).

INDEX